Jonathan Goodman has be  KU-628-340
as 'the premier investigator of crimes past'. He was editor
of the Celebrated Trials series and has written a number
of books on crime including *Murder in High Places* and
*Murder in Low Places*.

Jonathan Goodman is a member of the Medico-legal
Society and is one of the few lay members of the British
Academy of Forensic Sciences.

# THE LADY KILLERS

Famous women
murderers

*Edited by*

**JONATHAN GOODMAN**

SPHERE BOOKS LTD

A *Sphere* Book
First published in Great Britain by Judy Piatkus (Publishers)
Ltd 1990
This edition published by Sphere Books Ltd 1991
Copyright © This collection, Jonathan Goodman 1990

Reproduced, printed and bound in Great Britain by
BPCC Hazell Books
Aylesbury, Bucks, England
Member of BPCC Ltd.

ISBN 0 7474 0675 8

Sphere Books Ltd
A Division of
Macdonald & Co (Publishers) Ltd
Orbit House
1 New Fetter Lane
London EC4A 1AR

A member of Maxwell Macmillan Pergamon Publishing Corporation

*For the Reverend Peter Brierley – least of all because he is a collateral descendant of Florence Maybrick's Alfred*

# CONTENTS

# CONTENTS

# Deadly as the Male
### – an introduction

This is a collection of accounts of crimes, mainly of murder, that were certainly, probably or possibly committed by members of the gentle sex.

The *gentle* sex. . . . I shouldn't be surprised if some capital-F Feminist, one of those so ardent of the cause that they harm it, were to nominate me for insertion in a black list (or whatever such lists are now colour-unprejudicially called) or Men Who Look Down Upon Women – all because I, in my old-fashioned way, have revived the idea that her gender is gentle. Though that would be unfair (for I honestly do believe that a Ms is as good as a male in some respects, even better in some others), I hope it happens: there are few greater free and safe pleasures in life than to be given a reason all to oneself for exclaiming, 'Well, *there*,' about a long-savoured but meanwhile vicarious irritation. Come to think of it, The Angry Feminist would no doubt be perplexed – unsure whether her anger should be concentrated on the term 'the gentle sex' or on my associating of that term with murder. If she chose to be angry with me on the grounds that I have implied that murder*esses* are non-visibly different from murder*ers*, she would need to be careful, else she would confirm a gentleness of her sex so far as murder is concerned.

Gentleness? Well, yes – in that the firing of a dainty pistol or the administering of a subtle poison (which, if the annals of crime can be taken without salt, are the means to ends that have appealed to the majority of unaided and

1

undoubted murderesses) are, generally speaking, gentler methods of despatch than, say the whacking of vital parts of a body with an axe (which, I know, was the method used by Lizzie Borden, Kate Webster, and one or two other women – but they were exceptional to the common run of murderesses, who eschew methods that make a mess).

I don't know if there is anything in the old police adage that 'if poison is found, the poisoner's gown'd'; of course, there are statisticians who *claim* to know, but their sums of murders by both sexes are even more dubious than other sums to do with crime. There are several reasons for that:

For instance, because during the many years, till about the Second World War, when hardly a season passed without a person being tried for murder by poison, some of those persons, though guilty, were acquitted – and a few of the others were found guilty though, in fact, no crime had been committed. Even in those poison-trial-filled years, a comparatively considerable number of murders by poison went unsuspected or undetected or were unattributable; and during the nearly fifty years since those poison-trial-filled ones, there have been precious few poison trials (most British and American connoisseurs of crime in both Britain and America will, without having taxed their memories, recall the cases of Kenneth Barlow [English, a nurse, he gave his wife a lethal dose of insulin] and Carl Coppolino [American, an anaesthetist, he gave his wife a lethal dose of succinylcholine chloride], but will then, I bet, be stumped). The fact that poison trials have become rare is notwithstanding another fact: that bathroom cabinets, which have always usually been left-over medicine chests as well, are now less likely to contain bottles not quite emptied of Elliman's Royal Universal Embrocation or J. Collis Browne's Mixture for the Treatment of Diarrhoea and Coughs than remnants of prescribed barbiturates, amphetamine, heartbeat accelerators or decelerators, and/or of other artful pharmaceuticals that may be misused by people who are silly, shortsighted, suicidal – or murderous. It is not that murder by poison has almost died out, but that, for a long time now, a lot

2

of poisoners have got away with murders that either no one influential was suspicious about or no one influential was so suspicious about as to conduct, request or order an investigation.

Not all of the accounts comprising this collection are of poison cases. Of the eight that are, one, of the unsolved Balham Mystery, is by an American author who uses 'a-Priory' reasoning towards as firm a conclusion as to whodunit as that of certain British authors who have plumped for someone else; and another is of a case that many people at the time insisted, and some people now insist, put a woman in jeopardy of being hanged for a murder that never was; and another is of a case in which the only person who died was the servant-girl found guilty of the crime.

A number of women who would be apt to a collection of this sort are absent – some because they have been given their due in earlier volumes of this series.[1] For instance:

The aforementioned Lizzie Borden (who, after her orphaning, refined her forename to Lizbeth; I don't think that sparked the tale of the girl called Lizbeth who was one of 'leven children of a 'lectrician); Maria Barberi, who made literal use of a cut-throat razor; the self-made bridge-widow, Myrtle Bennett; Hannah Dustan, the tit-for-tat scalper of redskins. Those four are among *The Pleasures of Murder*. Christiana Edmunds, she of the bitter sweet, appears in *The Seaside Murders*; Adelaide Bartlett ('Birdie' to her Reverend boyfriend, who himself took flight, the minute she was accused of having poured neat chloroform into her husband) is in *The Christmas Murders*; and Constance Kent, who committed an awful crime in the almost-as-awful setting of an outside privy, is in *The Country House Murders*.

Having named and given the this-series whereabouts of those ladies, it is time, I think, to ask a rhetorical question:

Shall we join some others?

*Jonathan Goodman*

[1]Published in hardback by Allison & Busby (W.H. Allen), London, and in paperback by Sphere, London.

# The Lady's Not for Spurning
### Molly Tibbs

When Mrs Jean Harris hugged her dogs goodbye and drove away to an engagement with death, her life was a shattered mirror, a mere handful of dust. Everything had gone wrong, and there was no one to turn to.

The lonely 500 miles from Virginia to Westchester, New York, ticked past. As she drove the blue Chrysler through that night of Monday, 10 March 1980, she sat erect, like an automaton, small neat hands clenched on the wheel, a small sour smile sometimes flickering on her tight white face. Her mental anguish was extreme:

> *I am gall, I am heartburn. God's most deep decree*
> *Bitter would have me taste.*[1]

She was not entirely alone; for company, she had a loaded Harrington & Richardson .32 calibre revolver which she had bought in Virginia some eighteen months before.

Her destination was the expensive, Eastern pagoda-style home – all in the best possible taste – of Dr Herman Tarnower, her ancient lover, inventor of the famous Scarsdale Diet with its cruel repetition of grapefruit and spinach. Really, a better emblem for his affluence and contentment would have been the pair of stone grapefruits flanking the gates of his estate, rather than the concrete Buddha (a monster dwarf) on its eyot set

[1]From an untitled sonnet by Gerard Manley Hopkins.

in the pond, fringed with daffodils, on which, in happier days, the seamed and costive doctor would row her in his boat of love.

Once, he had promised her marriage, but he was a constant bachelor, ever a busy man of affairs. Carelessly, he plied her with amphetamines when she lost her sparkle. During the fourteen years of their relationships, she had never looked at another man, and he had never failed to look at another woman. She had swallowed hard and accepted whatever manna came her way, always careful to keep her independence. Her latest position was as headmistress of the exclusive Madeira School, in McLean, Virginia; it was no sinecure, but the status was satisfactory. Her marriage to James Scholes Harris, an ordinary man, had ended in 1965 after one of those matrimonial disagreements so curiously prevalent in our society over toothbrushes. She had brought up her two sons on her own, extremely well.

Now Jean Harris was fifty-six, a small, sharp, smart, svelte person, riddled with anger at those who wronged her – and at herself. Prickly, awkward in her interpersonal relationships, not precisely paranoid, but a *personalitas sensitiva*, she was quick to take offence, unable to tolerate criticism, intolerant of authority figures, particularly Madeira's board of directors (and, later, corrections officers). None of these quirks made her a bad person, and no one has ever claimed that Mrs Harris was a bad teacher, but the writing was on the blackboard for her at the school. Even worse, one of her rivals in Dr Tarnower's affections had, after some ten years of obscurity, stepped out of the chorus-line into her own cherished place as hostess at his gourmet dinner parties and companion on exotic holidays.

The usurper was Mrs Lynne Tryforos, divorced, at the elbow of the pond-owning doctor as his nurse-secretary at the Scarsdale Clinic. She was thirty-seven, not a bimbo, but Jean Harris certainly felt the age difference. Of late, an undignified, farcical situation had developed at the Tarnower homestead, where the two women's personal effects – especially sensitive articles such as negligées – were quickly shovelled out of sight in a box-and-cox arrangement. There was some besmirching and slashing of dresses going on, too. There is no doubt that the younger woman was winning and that Mrs Harris had become a non-person in Dr Tarnower's estimation. Testamentary considerations also obtruded.

Grimly, she drove onwards through the night. It was raining. 'Function in disaster, finish in style' was the Madeira motto. The pagoda house on Purchase Street was dark and unwelcoming at 11 p.m., even though she had told the doctor that she was coming to see him (she said). 'Suit yourself,' had been his memorable reply. Up the spiral stairs from the garage, stumbling slightly, into the bedroom where he was asleep. (Slowing down at the age of sixty-nine, he had retired two hours ago after entertaining to dinner Mrs Lynne Tryforos – who else? – and another friend.) 'Jesus, it's the middle of the night,' he grumbled as the light woke him. We are relying now on the Harris testimony, but the dialogue surely rings true.

Only Jean Harris knows – and lives with – what happened next, but the facts are these: that after some frightful scene, the doctor lay dying, bleeding to death, with four bullet wounds, and she was alive.

What she intended, and what she enacted, are not necessarily synonymous. On the journey to Westchester, she may not have had a fixed purpose, such were her ambivalent feelings towards Dr Tarnower. To contemplate a death, to arm oneself for a death, is not inevitably to proceed to its commission.

Mrs Harris is adamant that her intention was suicide: to shoot herself (spookily, in pitch darkness) beside the pond, 'where the weeping willow used to be' – to end it all, a sad Ophelia, where 'a willow grows aslant the brook'. Before that frightening event, she planned to have a last quiet, pleasant few minutes with the doctor, but *not* to tell him what she was going to do, *not* to ask *him* to shoot *her*, and *not* to shoot herself in front of him.

The imagined last scene of peace and reconciliation did

6

not come off. No words of comfort were offered. The Buddha was of stone, or concrete, and she, thwarted, disconcerted, wandered into the bathroom, where she found a greenish-blue satin negligée – *not hers* (so *was* she expected?) – which she hurled into the bedroom, closely followed by a box of curlers, which broke a window. He hit her. (Never before.) She threw a box. He hit her again. (Her face *was* bruised.) Then, 'I put my hair behind my ears and I raised my face to him and I closed my eyes and said, 'Hit me again, Hy, make it hard enough to kill. . . . ' It was very quiet, and I got up, I think to go, and I picked up my pocket-book and I felt the gun and I unzipped the bag, and I took out the gun and I said, 'Never mind, I'll do it myself,' and I raised it to my head and pulled the trigger at the instant that Hy came at me and grabbed the gun and pushed my hand away from my head and pushed it down, and I heard the gun explode. . . . Hy jumped back and I jumped back and he held up his hand and it was bleeding and I could see the bullet hole in it and he said, "Jesus Christ, look what you did."'

Now the story becomes more obscure, but the essence of it is that as the doctor tried to prevent her from shooting herself, during the struggle, he received the fatal wounds. Then she put the revolver to her head, 'And I shot and I shot and I shot and I shot and I shot and it just clicked.'

So there it was – a tragic accident and a failed suicide. Many areas of ambiguity remained, however, and the authorities of New York State interpreted the events as premeditated murder, even if there was also an intent to commit suicide after the deed (which would explain the will and other valedictory papers which Mrs Harris had left behind at Madeira – unless, of course, they were part of a plan to demonstrate pure suicidal intent). The death-wish appeared to have evaporated, her mind became wonderfully concentrated, when her trial formally began in Westchester on 21 November 1980; she passed documents to her attorney when he was on his feet as if she were an experienced member

7

of his team. Even so, a reckless person, she was prone to outbursts of rage and impatience at the legal process.

Joel Aurnou, her lawyer, showed himself to be the old-fashioned, flamboyant type of advocate, not embarrassed to weep at his client's predicament. When both Jean Harris and Aurnou chokingly explore the significance of her haunting epitome of herself – 'I was a person sitting in an empty chair' – there is scarcely a dry eye in the house. Her tears are observed to be reserved for herself – however she may mourn the doctor in private – and her demeanour is entirely wrong, misjudged. It is all right to be dignified, but to give an impression of arrogance is not clever at all. Even in England, it is not out of order for a lawyer to pay attention to the presentation of his client in court, and, behind the scenes, Aurnou and his phalanx of aides must have been trying to impress on their touchy client the difference between righteous anger at the charge, and a hard, shell-like disdain.

Much of the forensic evidence centred around the nature of the wounds in Dr Tarnower's hand and chest, with George Bolen, the young assistant district attorney, striving to show that they were defensive, that one bullet had passed through the doctor's hand *and into his chest* – but the expert witnesses effectively cancelled one another out.

However, it was not science, eventually, that the trial turned upon, but rather a product of the emotions, flimsy yet immensely powerful – the famous 'Scarsdale Letter'. Over the weekend before black Monday, 10 March, Mrs Harris had composed a denunciatory letter to Dr Tarnower, 'an anguished wail, held back for many years', and, on the Monday morning, she had posted it to him by registered mail, requiring the recipient's signature, 'because so many things I had sent him in the past had mysteriously never arrived'. Shortly after he had been instructed, Joel Aurnou fervently sought to retrieve that letter from the postal system. He argued that a person intent on killing someone on a certain day does not, on that same day, post a letter to the victim for him to sign for, and read, *on the following day*. He did capture the letter, against prosecution opposition, but it proved to be a two-edged sword.

Read aloud in Bolen's correctly neutral tones, in the course of cross-examination, it is supposed to have alienated the jury because it demonstrated a vicious motive for murder and also shattered one of the platforms for the defence – that Mrs Jean Harris was a fine lady and incapable of the crime for that reason. Let us look at the 'Scarsdale Letter':

Hy,

I will send this by registered mail only because so many of my letters seem not to reach you – or at least they are never acknowledged so I presume they didn't arrive.

I am distraught as I write this – your phone call to tell me you preferred the company of a vicious, adulterous psychotic was topped by a call from the Dean of Students ten minutes later and has kept me awake for almost thirty-six hours. I had to expel four seniors just two months from graduation and suspend others. What I say will ramble but it will be the truth – and I have to do something besides shriek with pain.

Let me say first that I will be with you on 19 April because it is right that I should be.[1] To accuse me of calling Dan to beg for an invitation is all the more invidious since it is indeed what Lynne does all the time – I am told this repeatedly, 'She keeps calling and fawning over us. It drives us crazy.' I have and never would do this – you seem to be able to expiate Lynne's sins by dumping them on me. I knew of the honour being bestowed on you before I was ever asked to speak at Columbia on the 18th.[2] Frankly I thought you were waiting for Dan's invitation to surprise me – false modesty or something. I called Dan to tell him

[1] An important dinner was to be given by the Westchester Heart Association in honour of Dr Tarnower on 19 April. Dan Comfort, a friend of the doctor, was organising the dinner.
[2] Mrs Harris had been invited to participate in a seminar at Columbia University, New York City, on 18 April.

I wanted to send a contribution to be part of those
honouring you and I assured him I would be there.
He said, 'Lee and I want you at our table.' I thanked
him and assured him I would be there 'even if the slut
comes – indeed, I don't care if she pops naked out
of a cake with her tits frosted with chocolate!' Dan
laughed and said, 'And you *should* be there and we
want you with us.' I haven't played slave for you –
I would never have committed adultery for you –
but I have added a dimension to your life and given
you pleasure and dignity, as you have me. As Jackie
[a mutual friend] says, 'Hy was always a marvellous
snob. What happened?' I suppose my cheque to Dan
falls into the 'signs of masochistic love' department,
having just, not four weeks before, received a copy
of your will, with my name vigorously scratched out,
and Lynne's name in *your* handwriting written in three
places, leaving her a quarter of a million dollars and her
children $25,000 apiece – and the boys and me nothing.
It is the sort of thing I have grown almost accustomed
to from Lynne – that you didn't respond to my note
when I returned it leaves me wondering if you sent
it together. It isn't your style – but then Lynne has
changed your style. Is it the culmination of fourteen
years of broken promises, Hy – I hope not. 'I want to
buy you a whole new wardrobe, darling.' 'I want to get
your teeth fixed at my expense, darling.' 'My home is
your home, darling.' 'Welcome home, darling.' 'The
ring is yours forever, darling. If you leave it with me
now I will leave it to you in my will.' 'You have, of
course, been well taken care of in my will, darling.' 'Let
me buy an apartment with you in New York, darling.'

It didn't matter all that much, really – all I ever
asked for was to be with you – and when I left you
to know when we would see each other again so there
was something in life to look forward to. Now you are
taking that away from me too and I am unable to cope
– I can hear you saying, 'Look, Jean, it's your problem
– I don't want to hear about it.'

I have watched you grow rich in the years we have

been together, and I have watched me go through moments when I was almost destitute. I have twice borrowed fifty cents from Henri[1] to make two of the payments on the Garden State Parkway [toll] during those five years you casually left me on my hands and knees in Philadelphia, and now – almost ten years later – now that a thieving slut has the run of your home, you accuse me of stealing money and books, and calling your friend to beg for an invitation. The very things your whore does openly and obviously (to your friends and your servants! sadly not to you) you now have the cruelty to accuse me of. My father-in-law left me a library of over five thousand books. I have given away in the past ten years more books than you own. I have thanked you most sincerely and gratefully for books you have given me. Ninety per cent of them have been given to a school library and on at least four different occasions I have asked you if you wouldn't like a letter on school stationery that you could use as a tax deduction. Each time you have airily refused and *now*, for God's sake, you accuse me of *stealing* your books. It borders on libel. Any time you wish to examine my home or the school library, you are certainly welcome to do so – a surprise raid might be most convincing for you.

Twice I have taken money from your wallet – each time to pay for sick damage done to my property by your psychotic whore. I don't have the money to afford a sick playmate – you do. She took a brand new nightgown that I paid $40 for and covered it with bright orange stains. You paid to replace it – and since you had already made it clear you simply didn't care about the obscene phone calls she made, it was obviously pointless to tell you about the nightgown. The second thing you paid for (I never replaced it) was a yellow silk dress. I bought it to wear at Lyford Cay[2] several years ago. Unfortunately I forgot to pack

---

[1]Henri van der Vrekens, Dr Tarnower's chauffeur and gardener. His wife, Suzanne, was the doctor's cook-housekeeper.
[2]An exclusive club at Nassau, in the Bahamas.

it because it was new and still in a box in the downstairs closet. When I returned it was still in the box rolled up, not folded now, and smeared and vile with faeces. I told you once it was something 'brown and sticky'. It was, quite simply, Herman Tarnower, human shit! I decided, and rightly so, that this was your expense, not mine. As for stealing from you, the day I put my ring on your dresser my income *before taxes* was $12,000 per year. I had two children in private school. They had been on a fairly sizable scholarship until I told the school I wouldn't need it because we were moving to Scarsdale. It was two years before we got it back. *That* more than anything else is the reason David [Mrs Harris's elder son] went to Penn State instead of the Univ. of Pennsylvania. He loathed every minute of it – and there is no question that it changed his life. That you should feel justified and comfortable suggesting that I steal from you is something I have no adjective to describe. I *desperately* needed money all those years. I *couldn't* have sold that ring. It was tangible proof of your love and it meant more to me than life itself. That you sold it the summer your adulterous slut finally got her divorce and needed money is a kind of sick, cynical act that left me old and bitter and sick. Your only comment when you told me you had sold it (and less than two months before you had assured me you would get it from the safe so I could wear it again!) was, 'Look, if you're going to make a fuss about it, you can't come here any more. I don't need to have anyone spoil my weekend.' Too bad Somerset Maugham didn't get hold of us before he died. He could have come up with something to top a *Magnificent Obsession*.

You have never once suggested that you would meet me in Virginia at *your* expense, so seeing you has been at my expense – and if you lived in California I would borrow money to come there, too, if you would let me. All our conversations are my nickels, not yours – and obviously rightly so because it is I, not you, who needs to hear your voice. I have indeed grown poor loving

12

you, while a self-serving, ignorant slut has grown very rich – and yet you accuse me of stealing from you. How in the name of Christ does that make sense?

I have, and most proudly so – and with an occasional 'right on' from others – ripped up or destroyed anything I saw that your slut had touched and written her cutesie name on – including several books that *I* gave you and she had the tasteless, unmitigated gall to write in. I have refrained from throwing away the cheap little book of epigrams lying on your bed one day so I would be *absolutely sure* to see it, with a paper clip on the page about how an old man should have a young wife. It made me feel like a piece of old discarded garbage – but at least it solved for me what had been a mystery – what had suddenly possessed you to start your tasteless diatribes at dinner parties about how every man should have a wife half his age plus seven years. Since you never mentioned it to anyone under sixty-five, it made the wives at the table feel about as attractive and wanted as I did. Tasteless behaviour is the only kind Lynne knows – though to her credit she *is* clever and devious enough to hide it at times. Unfortunately it seems to be catching.

The things I know or profess to know about Lynne – except for what I have experienced first-hand – I have been told by your friends and your servants, mostly the latter. I was interested to hear from Vivian and Arthur's[1] next-door neighbour in Florida – I don't remember her name though I am sure Lynne does: 'I took her to lunch, she seemed so pathetic' – that you sat at table while I was there and discussed Lynne and her 'wonderful family – brother a Ph.D.' I can't imagine going out to dinner with you and telling my dinner partner how grand another lover is. I told the woman to ask you sometime why if her family is so fine, Lynne decided to sell her kids to the highest bidder and make you and your family the guardian of her children

---

[1] Arthur Schulte: Dr Tarnower's closest male friend. Vivian: Arthur's wife.

if she should die before they do. It must go down as a 'first' for a splendid family to do. My phone tells me this – that 'mysterious' caller. I hope to God you don't know who it is! Who pays him?

When my clothes were ripped to shreds Suzanne said, 'Madam, there is *only* one person who *could* have done it. You must tell him.' In my masochistic way I tried to downplay it in my note to you, although in all honesty it was so obvious you would know who did it. Instead you ignored it and went happily off to Florida with the perpetrator. Suzanne told me – and I would think would say so in court.

1. The clothes were not torn when she went into the chest to find something of Henri's on 'Wednesday or Thursday' while we were away.

2. On the Sunday morning before we came home Henri and Suzanne both saw Lynne drive hurriedly up to your house. They were outside and she did not see him. They saw her go in but not out.

3. Lynne knew you were coming home that evening and she would see you by 8:00 the next morning. What business did she have at your home that morning?

4. When I discovered the clothes destroyed, Suzanne was sitting in the dining-room at the wooden table right next to the door. I said, 'My God – Suzanne, come look,' and she was right there. When I called your slut to talk to her about it and see what she was going to do about it, she said, 'You cut them up yourself and blamed it on me.' That was the first time it occurred to me they had been 'cut', not ripped. Only someone with a thoroughly warped mind would decide that a woman with no money would ruin about one-third of her wardrobe for kicks. Suzanne still believes Lynne did it and I most certainly do, too. I think this is enough evidence to prove it in court!

The stealing of my jewellery I can't prove at all. I just know I left some things in the white ashtray on your dresser as I have for many years. When I thought of it later and called, Lynne answered the phone. When I called again and asked Suzanne

14

to take them and put them away, they were gone. I only hope if she hocked them you got something nice as a 'gift'. Maybe I gave you some gold cuff links after all and didn't know it. I didn't for one instant think Henri or Suzanne took them. I had *never* called Lynne at the office anonymously as you have accused me that grim November day in 1977. I had in fact called her at the office before I left and said, since I did not have her number and could not get it I would call her at the office every time I got an anonymous phone call if she did not immediately stop them. Within two weeks my 'mysterious' caller told me her number. I have had it ever since then. Every single time she changes it I get it. And yet *though I was the one being wronged* you refused to let me come see you that month because a lying slut had told you *I* was calling her. The thought of it had never crossed my mind. Her voice is vomitous to me. The next month I called her virtually every single night *only* because of your rotten accusation while she sat simperingly by, letting you make it. Not *once*, not *once* did Lynne answer the phone. At one, two, three in the morning it was her children who answered, very quickly, TV playing. Where does mumsie spend her nights? That she 'totally neglects her children' is something Henri and Suzanne have told me. That you admire her for it is sad. She uses them to write 'super doctor' cute notes. With that kind of training Electra [one of Lynne Tryforos's two daughters] is going to be ready to earn her own colour television any day now. I hope to God you're not the one who buys it for her. I don't think Lynne would mind too much as long as you didn't change your will. 'Stupid' is certainly not the word for Lynne. In that I was totally wrong. 'Dishonest, ignorant and tasteless,' but God knows not stupid. It would have been heart-breaking for me to have to see less and less of you even if it had been a decent woman who took my place. Going through the hell of the past few years has been bearable only because you were still there and I could be with you whenever I could get away from work, which seemed to be less and less. To be jeered at, and called 'old and pathetic' made me seriously consider borrowing $5,000 just before I left New York and telling a doctor to make me young again – to do anything but make me not feel like discarded trash. I lost my nerve because there was always the chance I'd end up uglier than before.

You have been what you very carefully set out to be, Hy – the most important thing in my life, the most important human being in my life, and that will never change. You keep me in control by threatening me with banishment – an easy threat which you know I couldn't live with – and so I stay home alone while you make love to someone who has almost totally destroyed me. I have been publicly humiliated again and again but not on 19 April. It is the apex of your career and I believe I have earned the right to watch it – if only from a dark corner near the kitchen. If you wish to insist that Lee and Dan invite Lynne, so be it – whatever they may tell you, they tell me and others that they dislike being with her. Dan whispers it to me each time we meet, 'Why weren't you here? Lee hates it when it's Lynne.' I always thought that taking me out of your will would be the final threat. On that I believed you would be completely honest. I have every intention of dying before you do, but sweet Jesus, darling, I didn't think you would ever be dishonest about that. The gulf between us seems wide on the phone but the moment I see you it's as though we had been together forever. You were so absolutely perfect over David's wedding and I will always be grateful. I wish fourteen years of making love to one another and sharing so much happiness had left enough of a mark that you couldn't have casually scratched my name out of a will and written in Lynne's instead. But for God's

16

sake don't translate that into begging for money. I would far rather be saved the trial of living without you than have the option of living with your money. Give her all the money she wants, Hy – but give me time with you and the privilege of sharing with you 19 April. There were a lot of ways to have money – I very consciously picked working hard, supporting myself, and being with you. Please, darling, don't tell me now it was all for nothing. She has you every single moment in March. For Christ sake give me April. T. S. Eliot said it's the cruellest month – don't let it be, Hy. I want to spend every minute of it with you on weekends. In all these years you never spent my birthday with me. There aren't a lot left – it goes so quickly. I give you my word if you just aren't cruel I won't make you wretched. I never did until you were cruel – and then I just wasn't ready for it.

Every woman of any spirit who has ever been rejected will recognise this letter – this catharsis – as the one that makes you feel better, but is *never posted*, if you have a wisp of hope that the man still cares for you. It is the ultimate turn-off, as every man will recognise. Yet Jean Harris *did* post it, although her peroration – 'For Christ['s] sake give me April' – is indicative of a residue of reckless hope. It is fair to say that it is the voice of a very desperate woman – as Jean Harris would eagerly agree.

The feminists who had adopted Jean Harris as the archetypal wronged, discarded woman of our society, and who had rather sweetly taken notes at her trial, are supposed to have been dismayed by the Scarsdale Letter, because its 'vituperation' damaged the integrity and sanctity of their candidate for martyrdom. A better way to claim the letter for the feminist cause would be to argue that it shows Jean Harris as the victim of the romantic fallacy. Her own story, *Stranger in Two*

17

*Worlds*,[1] is interlaced with passages which represent the romantic intensity of the affair, as she experienced it. For example: 'The late afternoon sun came through the lacy old curtains at the windows in such a special way that time stood still for a while, and I knew that for some hard to explain reason I would remember the moment all my life. I was far away from home, but Hy was there, and the light from the window reminded me of a scene from a Pasternak story, or of home when I was a little girl. I loved Hy for being part of the moment and for giving the moment to me.' Thus and thus she further embroiled herself, Titania-like, while the object of her passion *had rather have a handful or two of dried peas*.

As for her betrayal of the status of a fine lady, that was Aurnou's gloss, for she never pretended to be a refined person in twin-set and pearls (although she had a dubious predilection for touches of mink) but, in her own self-image, was, and is, an intellectual. The 'shrewish vituperation' is the voice of an educated woman with a marvellous gift for invective. One can imagine that Germaine Greer herself would laugh at, and admire, the notorious 'chocolate-frosted' mammarial reference.

Perhaps, then, because she was seen by the jury (who were not her peers) to be not a real lady but a haughty fake, they convicted her of murder in the second degree. On 20 March 1981, Judge Russell Leggett, sentencing her to jail for fifteen years to life, delivered himself of a truly remarkable epilogue, during which his voice was heard to break (thus irresistibly reminding English readers of the sentencing of Seddon by Mr Justice Bucknill):

Mrs Harris, in regard to my observations of you, I found you to be a brilliant, brilliant woman, and I am going to ask this: in regard to Mrs Harris in Bedford Hills, my feeling is that she can be a most useful person in that facility and help other people. Her brilliance can probably bring some light into some other women's lives because of any ignorance and lack

[1]Macmillan Publishing Company, New York, 1986.

of knowledge. . . . I think that she has so much to offer the women that are there that not to afford her that opportunity would be to deprive society and the other inmates in there of a very great advantage and a blessing. It's unhappy that you have to be sentenced, Mrs Harris, and the best I can say to you is, the best of luck to you. . . . I wish the events of 10 March 1980 hadn't occurred.

Those gallant and emotional words strengthened Jean Harris in her own estimation of herself, and the authorities, heeding the judge's recommendation, have allowed her a positive role, working on the special problems of children whose mothers are in prison, as the guiding spirit of the Children's Centre at Bedford Hills. It would be utterly wrong, however, to state that she has at last found the peace and reconciliation which eluded her. She ill endures the brutal reality of prison life, she has heart attacks, she still says she is wrongly convicted, and she is still an incorrigible, pining Ariel – 'Air is the one pure thing here. A lovely gift. There are opposite moments too, when for no overt reason a tidal wave of nothingness and emptiness washes over me, consumes me, and I am alone in vast space.'

In such terms of *anomie* did the alienated Romantic Hero depict his plight, but he was a dangerous model for Jean Harris. 'I was a person, and no one ever knew,' she complained. She kept telling the world how she *felt*, but all they wanted to know was what she had *done*.

# Devilish Dumplings

*Anonymous* (From a Newgate Calendar)

The extraordinary interest taken by the public in this case induces us to give it at considerable length, in order that its weight and bearings may be justly appreciated and considered. The propriety of the conviction of the unfortunate young woman was much questioned; and upon a careful perusal of its circumstances, we think that at the least it must be concluded that the case was attended with considerable doubt.

It appears that Elizabeth Fenning was born in the island of Dominica, in the West Indies, on 10 June 1793. Her father, William Fenning, was a native of Suffolk, and belonged to the first battalion of the 15th regiment of infantry. Her mother was a native of Cork, in Ireland: her parents were respectable, and she was married to Fenning in 1787, in her native town, where the regiment had been quartered. In 1790 they sailed from the Cove of Cork for the island of Barbados, and thence to Dominica.

In 1796 or 1797 the regiment came home, having suffered great mortality, and were quartered in Dublin. In 1802 Fenning solicited and obtained his discharge, with a certificate of his good character, which it appears he merited, as he rose to the rank of a non-commissioned officer; and he then came to London, and entered the service of his brother, a potato-dealer in Red Lion Street, Holborn, with whom he continued for three years, and afterwards lived as servant in a potato-warehouse in Red Lion Passage, where his correct conduct gave satisfaction

20

to three successive proprietors. His wife, for five years, worked for one upholsterer – a sufficient proof of her good conduct. They had ten children, all of whom, except the subject of this narrative, died young. At the age of fourteen, she was placed out in service to obtain her own living; and at the latter end of January, 1815, she was hired as cook in the family of a Mr Orlibar Turner, at No. 68, Chancery Lane, where she had not been above seven weeks when circumstances unhappily arose which led to the poor creature's being charged with an attempt to poison her master's family.

The facts of the case will be best explained by the following report of the trial.

Eliza Fenning was indicted at the Old Bailey, 11 April 1815, for that she, on 21 March, feloniously and unlawfully did administer to, and cause to be administered to, Orlibar Turner, Robert Gregson Turner, and Charlotte Turner, his wife, certain deadly poison (to wit, arsenic) with intent the said persons to kill and murder.

The case was stated by Mr Gurney; after which –

*Mrs Charlotte Turner deposed*: I am the wife of Mr Robert Gregson Turner, who is a law-stationer in Chancery Lane, in partnership with his father, Mr Orlibar Turner, who lives at Lambeth. About seven weeks before the accident, the prisoner came into my service as cook; and about three weeks after, I had occasion to reprove her, for I observed her, one night, go into the young men's room partly undressed. There were two young men, about seventeen or eighteen years old. I reproved her severely next morning for her conduct; and the excuse was that she went in to fetch the candle. I threatened to discharge her, but on her expressing sorrow for the offence, I forgave her, and she remained in my employment. During the subsequent month, I observed that she failed to pay me that respect which I considered due to me, and she appeared extremely sullen. About a fortnight before the transaction now charged against her, she requested me to permit her to make some yeast dumplings, saying that she was a capital hand at it; and she frequently subsequently

21

repeated the same request. On Monday, 20 March, she came to me in the dining-room, and again asked me to allow her to make some dumplings, and said that the brewer had brought some yeast; and I said that as that was the case she might make the dumplings the next day, although that was not the way in which I usually had them made, as I generally had the dough from the baker's.

On Tuesday morning I went into the kitchen according to my custom, and I bade the prisoner make a beef-steak pie for the young men before she made the dumplings, and she carried the pie to the baker's before kneading the dough. I gave her some directions as to the manner in which I liked the dumplings, and then went away. In about half an hour, however, I returned into the kitchen and I then found the dough placed before the fire to rise. I have another servant in my employment named Sarah Peer, but I am certain that she could not have entered the kitchen during the time occupied in the preparation of the dumplings, as she was engaged by my direction in a bedroom mending a counterpane. I was subsequently in and out of the kitchen two or three times, and I observed that the dough did not rise. It was in a singular shape; and it remained heavy all the time.

At about three o'clock we sat down to dinner, and there were six dumplings brought to table. I observed to Sarah Peer that they were black and heavy instead of their being white and light. My husband, Robert Gregson Turner, and his father, Orlibar Turner, sat down to dinner with me: I helped them to some dumplings, and took a small piece myself. I found myself affected in a few minutes after I had eaten it. I did not eat a quarter of a dumpling. I felt myself very faint – an excruciating pain, which increased every minute: it came so bad that I was obliged to leave the table – I went upstairs. I ate, beside the dumpling, a piece of rump-steak cooked by Eliza.

When I was upstairs I perceived my sickness increased, and I observed my head was swollen extremely. I retched very violently: I was half an hour alone, and wondered they did not come to my assistance. I found my husband and father very ill – both of them. I was very ill from half past three until about nine; the violence then abated, but did not cease. My head and my tongue and chest were swollen. We called in a gentleman who was near, and afterwards Mr Marshall, the surgeon. We applied for the nearest assistance we could get.

*Cross-examined by Mr Alley*: This happened about six weeks after the girl came to live with me. I have heard the prisoner herself was taken very ill.

*Orlibar Turner deposed*: I am the father of Robert Gregson Turner. On Tuesday, 21 March, I was at my son's house in Chancery Lane: I dined there. The dinner consisted of yeast dumplings, beef-steaks, and potatoes. After some time Mrs Turner left the room indisposed. At the time she left the room I did not know she was ill. Some time after, my son left the room, and went downstairs. I followed him very shortly. I met my son in the passage at the foot of the stairs: he told me that he had been very sick, and had brought up his dinner. I found his eyes exceedingly swollen. I said I thought it very extraordinary, and I was taken ill myself in less than three minutes afterwards. The effect was so violent, I had hardly time to go into the back yard before my dinner came up. I felt considerable heat across my stomach and chest, and pain: I never experienced any vomiting before like it, for violence; it was terrible indeed. It was not more than a quarter of an hour when my apprentice, Roger Gadsden, was very ill, in a similar way to myself. While we were sick I was repeatedly in the parlour and the back yard. My son was up and down the stairs at intervals; Gadsden, I believe, was in the kitchen below.

The prisoner gave no assistance. We were all alarmed: but it was discovered that she did not appear concerned at our situation. I did not observe the prisoner eat any of the dumplings. I had a suspicion of arsenic, and made a search the next morning. I then observed in the pan, in which the dumplings had been mixed, that there was a white powder, unlike flour, and I retained it in my possession until I gave it into the hands of Mr Marshall.

Arsenic had been kept in the drawer in the office, tied up in a paper very tightly, and labelled 'Arsenic, poison', in large characters. I saw the parcel there on 7 March, but not since that time. It was missed about a fortnight before 21 March. The prisoner may have seen the parcel, as she usually resorted to the drawer for paper to light her fires. After dinner I remarked that the knives with which the dumplings had been cut had changed colour. They turned black and they still remain so. I spoke to the prisoner about the dumplings on the Wednesday, and I asked her how she came to put anything into them so hurtful, but she answered that it was not in anything which she had prepared, but in the milk which Sarah Peer had brought in, and with which her mistress had ordered her to make the sauce. That milk had been used in the sauce only. The dumplings had been mixed with the milk which had been left at breakfast.

*Roger Gadsden said*: I am an apprentice to Mr Turner. I remember seeing the packet of arsenic in the drawer, and I missed it a day or two after 7 March. On Tuesday, 21 March, I went into the kitchen between three and four o'clock, and I observed a plate on the table, on which were a dumpling and a half. I had dined at two o'clock, but I took up a knife and fork, and was going to eat the dumpling, when the prisoner exclaimed, 'Gadsden, do not eat that; it is cold and heavy; it will do you no good.' I ate a piece about the size of a walnut, and there being some sauce in the boat, I sopped it up with a piece of bread and ate it. I then went into the office, and Mr Turner came there in about ten minutes after, and said he was very ill. About ten minutes after that I was taken ill, but not so ill as to vomit. I was sent off for Mr Turner's mother. I was very sick going and coming – I thought I should die. The prisoner had made yeast dumplings for supper the night before: I and Peer and the prisoner partook of them: they were quite different from these dumplings in point of colour and weight, and very good.

*Margaret Turner sworn*: I was sent for. When I arrived I found my husband, son, and daughter, extremely ill. The prisoner, very soon after I was there, was ill, and vomiting. I exclaimed to her, 'Oh, these devilish dumplings!' supposing they had done the mischief. She

24

said, 'Not the dumplings, but the milk, madam.' I asked her, 'What milk?' She said, 'The halfpenny-worth of milk that Sarah fetched, to make the sauce.' She said my daughter made the sauce. I said, 'That cannot be; it could not be the sauce.' She said, 'Yes; Gadsden ate a very little bit of dumpling, not bigger than a nut; but licked up three parts of a boat of sauce with a bit of bread.'

*Mrs Turner, jun., being recalled, said*: The sauce was made with the milk brought by Sarah Peer. I mixed it, and left it for her to make.

*Robert Gregson Turner sworn*: I partook of the dumplings at dinner; I ate none of the sauce whatever. Soon after dinner I was taken ill: I first felt an inclination to be sick; I then felt a strong heat across my chest. I was extremely sick; I was exactly as my father and wife were. I had eaten a dumpling and a half, and I suffered more than any other person. I should presume that the symptoms were such as would be produced by poison.

*Sarah Peer sworn*: I have been servant to Mrs Turner near eleven months. I recollect the warning given to the prisoner some time after she came. After that I heard her say she should not like Mr or Mrs Robert Turner any more. On 21 March I went for some milk after two o'clock, after I had dined with the prisoner on beef-steak pie. I had no concern whatever in making the dough for the dumplings, or in making the sauce. I was not in the kitchen when the dough was made: I never meddled with it, or put anything to it; I never was in the kitchen after I went up to make the beds, a quarter after eleven, until dinner time. I had permission to go out that afternoon, directly after I took up the dumplings. I went out directly. I came home at nine o'clock exactly. I ate none of the dumplings myself. In eating the beef-steak pie, I ate some of the crust. I was not at all ill. I had eaten some dumplings she had made the night before: I never tasted any better. They were all made out of the same flour. I had no difference with my mistress at any time.

*Cross-examined by Mr Alley*: I had occasionally quarrelled with the prisoner. I went sometimes to visit my friends, but it was generally on Sundays. I never went on a week-day except on this occasion. I know nothing of the drawer in which the arsenic was. The paper which I used for lighting fires was kept in the dining-room. I never went to the drawer in the office, nor did I ever see or hear of any poison being kept there.

An officer of Hatton Garden and the brewer's man were then successively examined. The first proved that on his apprehending the prisoner, she declared that she thought the poison must have been in the yeast, as she saw a red settlement in it after she had used it, and the second stated that the yeast was good, and that he delivered it to the girl Peer.

Mr John Marshall, a surgeon, was then sworn, and he stated that on his being called in to Mr Orlibar Turner's family he found them all labouring under symptoms of having taken arsenic, and that the prisoner was also ill, and exhibited similar symptoms. On the following day he saw a pan, and on his examining its contents he found them to contain arsenic. He had also examined the yeast which was left and the flour tub, and they were both devoid of arsenic. The poison being cut would blacken the knife.

The case for the prosecution being closed, the prisoner made the following defence:

'I am truly innocent of the whole charge; I am innocent; indeed I am. I liked my place, and was very comfortable. Gadsden behaved improperly to me; my mistress came and saw me undressed; she said she did not like it; I said, "Ma'am, it is Gadsden that has taken a liberty with me." The next morning I said, "I hope you do not think anything of what passed last night." She was in a great passion, and said she would not put up with it; I was to go away directly. I did not look upon Mrs Turner as my mistress, but upon the old lady. In the evening the old lady came to town; I said, "I am going away tonight." Mrs Turner said, "Do not think any more about it; I don't." She asked Mrs Robert Turner if she was willing for me to go. She said, "No, she thought no more about it." As to my master saying I did not assist him, I was too ill. I had no concern with that drawer at all; when I wanted a piece of paper, I always asked for it.'"

The prisoner called five witnesses, who gave her an excellent character for integrity, sobriety, cheerfulness, and humanity. One of them was proceeding to state an accidental conversation which he had with the prisoner two days after she had ordered the yeast, wherein she declared herself happy and contented with her situation, and pleased with her master and mistress; but the Recorder stopped him, saying it was not evidence.

Whilst the trial was proceeding, William Fenning, the father of the prisoner, went to a public-house, and got a person (for he was too agitated himself) to write on a slip of paper that on 21 March he went to Mr Turner's, his daughter having sent for him in the morning, and that Sarah Peer told him Eliza had gone with a message for her mistress, whilst, at the same time, she was in agonies below-stairs from the effect of having eaten of the dumplings. He then went home, and thought no more about it.

This note was handed to Mr Alley, who, standing upon tiptoe, showed it to the Recorder, who leaned over and looked at it, but no further notice was taken of it.

Other efforts were made by the prisoner to produce witnesses, but as they were not in attendance, the court said that it was too late, and that the trial could not be suspended for their coming.

The Recorder then proceeded to sum up the case, and the jury in a few minutes brought in a verdict of guilty. The Recorder having then passed sentence of death upon her, the miserable girl was carried from the bar convulsed with agony, and uttering frightful screams.

Few cases ever excited greater interest than that of Eliza Fenning; and we are happy in being able to state that her religious principles were correct, and her professions sincere. Through life she was distinguished by a superiority of intellect, and a propriety of deportment, which could hardly be reconciled with the depravity of which she was accused. In person she was short of stature, but of the most perfect symmetry; her countenance evinced a heart at ease, and a mind at once intellectual and lively. She had been before the fatal transaction betrothed to a young man, to whom she appears to have been sincerely attached.

After the unfortunate girl's conviction she was induced to apply to the Crown for a remission of the sentence of death, and sent a petition to the Prince Regent. She next addressed the Lord Chancellor, to whom she sent a statement of all the exculpatory circumstances of her case. She also sent a letter to Lord Sidmouth, and another to her late master, requesting him to sign a petition in her favour, with which however he refused to comply.

Several gentlemen interested themselves in the fate of the poor girl; and Mr Montagu, of Lincoln's Inn, waited on the Recorder, offering to produce evidence of a member of Mr Turner's family, who was insane, having declared that he would poison the family; but the Recorder assured him that the production of such evidence would be wholly useless.

The night before her execution, a meeting of gentlemen took place in Mr Newman's apartments in Newgate, at which Mr Gibson, of the house of Corbyn and Co., chemists, No. 300, Holborn, stated that Robert Gregson Turner, in the month of September or October, called at their house in a wild and deranged state, requesting to be put under restraint, otherwise he declared he should destroy himself and wife. Mr Gibson also stated that it was well known in the family that Robert Turner was occasionally subject to such violent and strange conduct.

With this information Mr Gibson, accompanied by a clerk from the Secretary of State's office, waited on the Recorder, requesting that the unfortunate girl might be respited to admit of investigation; but all was of no avail, and in twelve hours after, Eliza Fenning was executed.

From the moment the poor girl was first charged with the poisoning, however or by whomsoever questioned, she never faltered in her denial of the crime, and rather courted than shunned an investigation of her case. So many circumstances, which had developed themselves subsequently to the trial, had been communicated to the Secretary of State by the gentlemen who interested themselves in her favour (among whom were some of great respectability), that a reprieve was confidently expected to the last: and the order for her execution, four months after her conviction, was received with very great surprise.

On Tuesday morning, 25 July, she took her last farewell of her father, who, by the firmness of his manner, exemplified the courage he wished his child to sustain upon the scaffold: but with her mother the parting scene was heart-rending.

On the fatal morning, 26 July 1815, she slept till four o'clock, when she arose, and, after carefully washing herself, and spending some time in prayer, she dressed herself neatly in a white muslin gown and cap. About eight o'clock she walked steadily to the spot where criminals are bound; and, whilst the executioner tied her hands – even whilst he wound the halter round her waist – she stood erect and unmoved, with astonishing fortitude. At this moment a gentleman who had greatly interested himself in her behalf adjured her, in the name of that God in whose presence she was about to appear, if she knew anything of the crime for which she was about to suffer, to make it known; when she replied distinctly and clearly, 'Before God, then, I die innocent!' The question was again put by the reverend Mr Vazie, as well as by the Ordinary, and finally by Oldfield, a prisoner who suffered with her, and to each she repeated, 'I am innocent.' These were her last words; and she died without a struggle, at the age of twenty-one.

Her miserable parents, on application for her body, were not prepared to pay the executioner's fee of 14s 6d: but having borrowed the money with some difficulty, the remains of their daughter were handed over to them.

We have endeavoured to give the circumstances of this case as clearly and with as little prejudice as possible, but we should not do our duty if we were not to state that the public mind was much inflamed at the execution of the unhappy prisoner. Thousands of persons, after examining the evidence adduced at the trial, did not hesitate to express their opinions very strongly upon the subject of the case; and many of the lower orders, apparently convinced of the innocence of the sufferer, assembled in front of Mr Turner's house in Chancery Lane, hooting and hissing, and otherwise expressing their indignation, at what they conceived to be their unjust prosecution of their servant.

The police were active in their exertions to suppress the tumult; and an affidavit made by Davis, a turnkey in Newgate, was industriously circulated, in which the deponent swore that old Fenning had conjured his daughter, when she went upon the scaffold, to declare her innocence: a counter-affidavit of the father of the wretched girl, however, was produced and published, and the assertion of the jailer was at length admitted to have been founded upon a mistaken interpretation of what had really passed.

The mob continued to assemble for many days, and it was not until the police had taken very vigorous measures against them that they were finally dispersed. The public still sympathised with the unhappy parents of Eliza Fenning, and a subscription was entered into for their benefit.

# Mrs Costello Cleans the Boiler
### Edmund Pearson

Mrs Nellie Ayers, an aged peddler of candy, was known to many of her customers in Peabody, Massachusetts, as 'the fudge woman'. One morning in February 1933, intent on business, she called at the home of the Costellos. After a little sales talk, while patting the baby on the head, she entered into covenant with Mrs Jessie Costello for a pound of fudge.

That lady went upstairs for her purse, but immediately began to utter shrill screams.

'She screamed something terrible,' said the fudge woman in a later description.

The only other adult person on the ground floor of the house was a temporary helper, a Polish woman whose name ought to mean something, since she was called Mrs Simbolist. She did not hear the screams, possibly because she was busy with the favourite occupation in the Costello household: cleaning the kitchen boiler. And she was wiping her streaming eyes, as a result of trying to shine the copper with some curious hellbroth furnished by her employer. She had never used this stuff before.

Mrs Costello rushed downstairs again, exclaiming, 'Bill's dead!'

'And who,' enquired the fudge woman, 'may Bill be?'

'He's my husband,' cried the other, 'an' he's up there, lyin' on the floor, dead.'

'All of this,' replied the peddler of sweets, with some hauteur, 'is beside the question. Here's your fudge. Where's my money?'

31

'Oh, I couldn't,' moaned the young widow, 'I couldn't think of fudge now. With Bill up there dead an' all!'

'Madam,' said the majestic saleswoman, 'a bargain is a bargain. That's my last word to you.'

And she stalked across the street into a neighbour's house, where she explained her ideas of commercial honour.

'In my day,' said she, 'people kept their promises.'

She repeated this loud and long, and at last to reporters, so that her complaints reached the press, and her grievance became known throughout New England.

For the fudge woman, like many another innocent by-stander, had stumbled upon tremendous events; she had smelled the smoke of the fire that is never quenched. Bill's death had been sudden, its cause obscure, and into his house came neighbours and physicians, then detectives and pathologists.

Bill, officially known as Captain William J. Costello of the Peabody Fire Department, had returned early that morning from a night spent with a company of friends in the ancient rites of watching over the body of a deceased associate.

He had been in good health and spirits, quite the life of the wake. Partaking of ham sandwiches, pie, and coffee at midnight, he left at 2 a.m., promising to return in five hours. Even this short rest had not interested him, for – according to Mrs Costello – as soon as he got home he embarked upon the great family recreation of cleaning the boiler. Or, rather, of mixing the pestilential brew which – again according to Mrs Costello – was their familiar and favourite lotion for that purpose. The brightness of their boiler was the chief concern of the household; they rubbed it by day and muttered about it in their sleep. Once more, our informant is Mrs Costello.

Despite scandalous rumours, despite hundreds of newspaper articles, there was no immediate arrest. But the autopsy revealed that Captain Costello had cyanide of potassium in him. A detective learned that the night before the Captain's death, Mrs Costello had bought this substance, together with oxalic acid. Her mind, of course, was bent upon imparting a still greater radiance to the pride of the family, the kitchen boiler. Tales of neighbourhood scandals caused this detective to call upon the widow and ask if she had had any poison in the house.

'Absolutely not,' said she; 'devil a bit.'

But he pursued the subject.

'How about cyanide of potassium?'

'Oh, if you call that stuff poison!' she replied.

That is exactly what the Commonwealth of Massachusetts, in its prim, old-fashioned manner, does call potassium cyanide, and so for many pleasant days in the following July and August, a jury in Salem listened to Mrs Costello's explanations. The lid was taken off the section of Peabody where the Costellos lived, and the reek of neighbourhood gossip went up, as thick and poisonous as the fumes from the cauldron when Mrs Simbolist tried to clean the boiler.

The trial was conducted with a dignity, and at the same time a kind of antique simplicity that (as I like to think) would be found in few other places in America. In front of the solid and forbidding old court house there daily gathered a crowd, mainly of women and children, to watch the defendant arrive and alight from the sheriff's motor car. This group was kept within bounds, so that the street, and most of the sidewalks, were quite clear for traffic and passers-by.

Shortly before 10 a.m., the jury appeared, walking slowly, two by two. At the head of the column, and at its foot, went a tipstaff, in blue, and with brass buttons. Each of these officers carried a wand, about seven feet long, gilded at the end. The jury came from the Hawthorne Inn, where they had apparently spent a peaceful night. The hour after breakfast, between 9 and 10, was usually passed in Dr Phippen's garden, and on some days each juror wore a boutonnière. The day I saw them, these decorations were absent, but the tipstaves each solemnly carried, in addition to his wand, a big bouquet of flowers. Whether these were for judge or prisoner, or merely to decorate the jury room, I did not discover.

After the jury had gone inside, there drew into the street the sheriff's car, with two or three officers, and the defendant. Jessie Costello had become a personage, discussed from Eastport to Westport, a lady with a reputation for beauty and a talent for invective. To see her skip out of the limousine and run smiling into the court house, people waited for hours in the hot sun. To get one of the seats allotted to spectators, other people stood in line all night.

In the court room, people did not perch on windowsills, nor stand in the aisles. Thirty spectators were allowed to occupy seats, and no more than thirty were admitted. Reporters were restricted to their section. Judge and jury, lawyers and witnesses and officers had room to move and think and deliberate. The walls of the room, and the green-shaded windows, were tall and cool. The national flag and the beautiful gold and white emblem of the Commonwealth were on either side of the bench. The judge was austere and self-possessed: a typical judge of a State which does not require its justices to curry favour with the electorate, nor canvass for votes. Over his head was a full-length painting of Chief Justice Shaw, who delivered the famous charge in the trial of Professor Webster. And, on a blackboard near the witness-stand, a diagram, in chalk, of Bill Costello's stomach.

Among the women Massachusetts has tried for murder, one must go far back – probably to Bathsheba Spooner of revolutionary days – to match Mrs Costello in charm. Perhaps for the first time in her life, she was dressed in good taste; in black, with a big white jabot. Her figure was a trifle dumpy, and her slightly rolling gait could have been a waddle if she had not tripped in and out of court so merrily. Her clear white complexion might have seemed – after months in jail – too pallid, had she not corrected this, very skilfully, with her only cosmetic, a little rouge. Her dark eyes, under heavy unplucked eyebrows, were her best feature. For a few days, many of the reporters were highly appreciative of these fascinating eyes, until, one morning, they saw them narrow like a snake's and her whole countenance harden with anger at a cameraman, as

she spat at him the single – and inappropriate – word:
'Bitch!'

But let not those who have never been hounded by press photographers chide Mrs Costello. She made no pretence of agreeing that 'No Nice Girl Swears', and the charge of using 'vulgar, profane, and blasphemous language' urged against her by witnesses for the prosecution is the only one she did not deny.

'Never in the presence of the children,' was all that she said.

Mrs Costello, as the trial progressed, emerged as the only truth-teller in court. The people who perjured themselves, in great matters or small, included some of her own witnesses and friends, as well as witnesses for the State. For instance, the pharmacist who sold her the cyanide warned her that it was deadly stuff, and she replied that she knew all about it. But in her testimony she declared that she never knew it was harmful until Bill died.

His fellow-firemen and his friends at the wake bore witness to Bill's sound health and spirits, but his widow assured the jury that he was mentally decayed and physically feeble – quite in the mood to seek death (although a pious Catholic) by gulping down a big hooker of boiler polish.

'They'll have to go like hell to find any poison in Bill with all that embalming fluid in him.'

This remark, as the autopsy drew near, was attributed to Mrs Costello. But the lady denied it, and a male relative gallantly assumed the blame for this cynicism.

Medical testimony suggested that the poison was administered in a capsule, probably under pretence that it was some simple medicine, appropriately taken the morning after a wake. Mrs Costello denied all knowledge of capsules. She didn't even know what they looked like. And then a neighbour, Mrs Bisson, most unwillingly testified that she had seen Mrs Costello buy and fill capsules in an earlier instance of private doctoring.

A curious incident in the trial was the appearance of the manager of a local moving-picture theatre to testify

35

that the film being shown just before the tragedy was *Payment Deferred*.[1] It was suggested by the defence that this might have given Costello the idea of self-destruction by cyanide. But the theme of that play is murder, and the expression in the eyes of Charles Laughton as he watched his nephew die of cyanide would hardly attract anyone to this form of death.

The contention of the State was that Mrs Costello had a waning regard for her husband, an excessive interest in his insurance money, as shown when she went to the fire station to collar his policies before his body was in the coffin, and, most of all, an undue passion for a neighbour – young Patrolman McMahon of the Peabody police.

This officer was called in hundreds of headlines the 'Kiss-and-Tell Cop'. Kiss was but a schoolgirl's feeble euphemism for what happened, but tell he certainly did. Before the grand jury, he perjured himself like a gentleman, and everyone seemed to approve. Then, either the influence of religion caused him to fear hellfire or the power of the law made him dread being included in the indictment. For upon the witness stand he recited a tale which put the record of the trial on the *Index Librorum Prohibitorum*, and sounded more like a fourteenth-century Florentine frenzy than the annals of Essex County, Massachusetts.

Reporters stopped writing about the Salem witches – who were tried right around the corner – and began references to Hester Prynne and the big, big Scarlet Letter.

It was a pickup, on the street, while McMahon was directing the Peabody traffic. Up drove the fatal Jessie in her car, with a very glad eye and the invitation, 'How would you like to be in here?'

[1]EDITOR'S NOTE: The screen version of the play (the West End and Broadway premieres of which, both in 1931, had also starred Charles Laughton) adapted by Jeffrey Dell from C.S. Forester's novel – which was inspired by a murder-may-have-been-suicide theory put forward by counsel for Herbert Rowse Armstrong at his trial (Herefordshire Winter Assizes, 1922) for the murder of his wife. Edgar Wallace's account of the Armstrong poisoning case appears in *The Country House Murders*, Allison & Busby, London, 1987.

After that, it was all up with Officer McMahon. While Captain Costello was on duty at the fire station, there were stolen rides to convenient parking places along the Newburyport Turnpike, as well as many trysts in the Costello home. When his wife went to a hospital, poor McMahon was seized, like the Sabine women, and carried off to dwell with the Costellos. Even when he sought respite in an appendicitis operation, and retired to the hospital, there was no leave of absence. The determined Jessie visited him every evening, and strained the rules of the hospital by the length of her calls. Her family physician, one Dr Pomeroy, a rather curious figure in the case, found her hiding one night behind the door of McMahon's room, and curtly bade her cease her foolishness and come out.

More angered by the recital of the love affair than by the charge of murder, Mrs Costello rushed to the witness stand to deny it all, lock, stock, and barrel, and call Eddie McMahon seven kinds of copper-riveted liar. Why, she barely knew the fellow; her friendship with him, like that of Bunthorne with the vegetables, was merely a passion à la Plato.

McMahon, by the way, was soon out of the Police Department, but it was one of the charming oddities of the case that he was offered and accepted a job with Lydia Pinkham, the woman's friend.

Nobody suggested any reason why McMahon should invent the story he told on the witness stand, but the man in the street denounced him as a yellow dog. The same eminent man in the street listened to Mrs Costello's tarradiddles and admired her for them.

'Of course, she had to say that!'

Truth is not highly esteemed in our courts of law; perjury, from most of the witnesses, seems to be expected as a matter of course.

The jury brought in an acquittal. Many people were astonished, but they cynically attributed the verdict to the fact that twelve male jurors sat for weeks in close proximity to the prisoner, and as helpless as twelve rabbits under the influence of those glittering ophidian

eyes. This may be unjust. Perhaps they relied on the
ancient belief that 'a woman couldn't do such a thing'
and that when the woman was, moreover, the mother
of young children, the charge must be preposterous. Or,
perhaps, the State tried to prove too much: it certainly
allowed one of its medical witnesses to introduce a
complicated argument on a pathological subject. It was
as interesting, and as involved, as a chapter in one of Mr
Austin Freeman's detective novels but, unfortunately,
was irrelevant to the point at issue.

Broadway had a brief glimpse of Mrs Costello, but
offered her no theatrical engagement. Her partnership
with Mrs Aimee Semple McPherson, the evangelist of
Angelus Temple, was likewise brief.

To us home-lovers, who admire the New England
housewife and her traditional love of cleanliness, the
really important thing was to have Jessie at home once
more. The kitchen boiler had been neglected for months,
and nothing seemed so appropriate as to let Mrs Costello
and her lawyers give it a good polish. Especially with
that widely used and reliable preparation, cyanide of
potassium.

# The Widow of Windy Nook
## Richard Whittington-Egan

The very name of the place where the widow had her arachnidan lair, Windy Nook – a village embedded now in Felling, a dour suburban stretch on the south bank of the Tyne, just beyond the tentacled embrace of Gateshead – sets pictures flickering through the mind. A monochrome scene, grained and jerky like a thirties' film. A miserly terrain that bore and shaped likewise stunted men and women, thin-lipped from long compression, hard-stone-eyed from want.

It was this chill east side of the industrial North Country that begat that terrible Victorian bogeywoman, Mary Ann Cotton, secret poisoner supreme. This is the story of another Mary from County Durham: Mary Elizabeth Wilson. But before she was Mrs Wilson she bore three different surnames, baptismal and married. You see marriage, for Mary, was a habit; and a very bad habit for her husbands. There were four of them, counting-in one of the so-called 'common law' variety. This is the story of a classic poisoning case, one of the last of the old-fashioned vintage murders when hanging was still a possibility.

It is 1914. Mary is twenty-two and newly wed. Her husband, John Knowles, had been the son of the house where she was employed as a domestic servant. Those were the times when even the only moderately well-to-do could afford to keep an underpaid, overworked drudge. She must have seen the match as self-betterment. Not that John Knowles was ever to amount to much. He found work, and his level, as a labourer. He neither aspired nor ascended. The marriage was not, by all accounts, a happy one, perhaps because Mary's husband was such a bad-tempered man. Nevertheless, it, and she, endured. It lasted for over forty years. Nominally, anyway. As one commentator felicitously put it, 'They remained living under the same roof, although not on the same mattress.'

In fact, a marital escape hatch had opened in the brush-flaunting shape of a chimney sweep. It is an old North Country superstition that to meet a sweep going to or from the church on your wedding day is very lucky. In Mary's case, the meeting with John George Russell, sweep, long after her wedding day, certainly seemed lucky to her. He arrived at the Knowles' as an innocent lodger, but had soon graduated to Mary's bed. In such a state of sexual truce, the marriage defied the traps and perils imported by the years. 'As long as Knowles' meals arrived on the table in good time, and his shirts, socks and other laundry were washed, aired and put away in the old-fashioned chest of drawers, he was apparently content,' is how the late Leonard Gribble, writer, most neatly summarised the status quo.

The year is now 1955. Mrs Mary Knowles is still an ordinary – albeit sexually beleaguered – North Country housewife, aged sixty-three. She is a plain, pinkish-cheeked, rather stout and homely person with tight-curlered, ginger-grey hair and flintily bright calculating eyes. It is a guarded and ungiving face. Mary is a self-possessed woman known to be grasping, earthy in a North Country way, addicted to trashy romantic magazines and paperback novelettes and even more addicted to the bottle. Hardly a *femme fatale* but, as events were to prove, there must have been *some* quality of magnetism there.

For forty-one years this unprepossessing matron maintained a relatively normal balance. Then something changed . . . or broke. She found within herself a dreadful potential – a terrifying, cruel capacity – for evil.

40

It was in the early summer that Mary discovered Rodine, the would-be widow's friend. In July her husband fell sick. In August he died.

The flowers on John Knowles' grave had barely withered before his grieving widow began to confide to the ears of her sympathising neighbours her feeling that it was time she had a change. In fact, she intimated, her late husband had agreed with her about the desirability of making a move. That was just before he died. Now, after what had happened, with the sad memories clinging to what had been their home for many years, she really did want to leave. The neighbours nodded in sage and sympathetic understanding. Of course, poor thing.

And so she moved. Not far, but to a new house, a new start. Well . . . almost. There was still one more change pending.

John Russell, her long-time lover-lodger, she took with her. Not however, without duly warning, 'I may have to put up the rent. But that's only because things are more pricey now. Otherwise, everything will be just the way it was before.' Lies.

Autumn came. The moors turned brown and gold. Then winter, early, pencilling the land with tracings of frost and snow. The cold winds blew. At Christmas it was John Russell's turn to take to his bed – alone. The unfestive fact was that Mary, having found how easy it was to dispose of the unwanted man in her life, and finding another now not wholly welcome, decided to try again. She seemed determined to make, as it were, a clean sweep. Russell's indisposition worsened. Before January 1956 was out, so was he.

It may have struck the good people of Windy Nook that there was something a bit strange, a bit fishy, about two men who had lived in the same house dying in quick succession like that. But it passed as coincidence. Folk up there were used to the good Lord's little jokes. And after all, they *were* both old men, and the doctor *had* certified natural causes. Moreover, both men were of humble station in life, and the terrible thing is that once they had been translated into anonymous humps on the smooth sward of the Durham burying-ground, the community within which they had been known for most of their lives soon forgot that they had ever lived.

With Johns *primus* and *secondus* both dead within five months, the double widow promptly set about the sanitary dusting away of memories. She had her late lover's room refurbished. Fresh paint. Bright new wallpaper. 'It isn't as though he passed away because he had anything contagious or infectious, is it? But you can't take chances with health, I always say,' she explained to her street acquaintances.

Spring and the primroses arrived. Pale sunlight intensified, deepened, and grew warmly stronger. The widow's weeds blossomed seductively. Mary was on the husband hunt again. . . .

That summer she was introduced to Oliver James Leonard, estate agent, retired. Seventy-six years of age. He lodged with the Widow Knowles' friends, Mr and Mrs Connelly, at Hebburn-on-Tyne, about four miles east of Gateshead. Plainspeaking and crude, Mrs Knowles did not mince her words. 'Has the old bugger any money?' she asked Mrs Connelly. 'A little, so far as I know,' was the reply that sealed Mr Leonard's fate.

The Widow Knowles was a fast worker. That same week, lamb to the slaughter, Leonard was off to lodge with her. He was not all lamb, though. He was of a bossy nature. A row blazed. Three days later, Mrs Knowles was knocking on Alice Connelly's door, demanding that she take back her annexed lodger. 'He won't sign any money over to me until he puts a ring on my finger,' she shouted angrily. 'So get the old bugger out.'

Eventually avarice triumphed and peace was made. On the first day of autumn – 21 September – at Jarrow Registry Office, Mary and Oliver were married.

For love or money, Mary does not seem to have been able to make a success of matrimony. Within days of the wedding Mr Leonard was poorly with a shocking cold. And before he had time to recover, he was dead.

It was late on Wednesday night, 3 October – that Mrs Ellen Russell, a neighbour, was awakened by the new

Mrs Leonard with the news that her husband was ill.
Mrs Russell went back to Mrs Leonard's house with
her. They found the old man on the floor, white-faced,
speechless, breathing heavily and in obvious pain. That
universal panacea, a nice strong cup of tea, was brewed
in a trice. Offered it, Mr Leonard knocked the cup out of
Mrs Russell's hand.

'I think he's dying,' was that astonished lady's reaction.

'I think so, too,' said Mrs Leonard quickly. Adding,
'I've called you because you'll be handy if he does.'

He did.

The following day the widow reported his death to their
GP, Dr Laydon. The doctor remembered that the old
man had come to see him the previous day for treatment
for a bad cold. Obviously it was a case of senility. No
need to see the body. With a clear conscience he filled
in a death certificate – (1) Myocardial degeneration. (2)
Chronic nephritis.

His widow collected £75, which was all he had had.
When Leonard's son – with whom, admittedly, he had
been on bad terms – came calling to see his father's will,
Mary sent him packing with a flea in his ear. 'Go and see
the solicitor,' she told him sharply. (It is extraordinary
how often murderers and murderesses are tactlessly
abrupt with the relatives of their victims, as witness the
cases of Seddon and the Vonderahes, the Stauntons and
Mrs Butterfield, and George Joseph Smith's gratuitously
offensive response to a solicitor acting for the family of
one of his victims.)

It was not long before Mary was casting a glittering
eye around for a new husband. The black widow was
hungry for another mate, a money-spider, to devour
and suck dry. She looked hard and took her time; a
full twelvemonth. Then she set her rakish widow's cap
at another old man . . . and pounced.

Ernest George Lawrence Wilson, a 75-year-old retired
engineer, had let it be known that he was looking for a
housekeeper. What was on offer to the right applicant,
he hinted, was a tidy little £100 investment in the Co-op,
a paid-up insurance policy, and a nice home. When these

tidings came to the voracious ear of our Mary, she made hasty investigation. Investment and policy must have passed muster, but the nice home turned out to be a dirty council bungalow, rented for 6s 6d. a week. The closer Mr Wilson came into focus, the less dazzling appeared the benefits and inducements on offer. Not withstanding, possibly with a short-term policy well in mind, Mary Leonard accepted, sold up her furniture and went to live at the bungalow in Rectory Road, Windy Nook, with Wilson.

On 30 October 1957, they were married.

The wedding was by no stretch of the imagination a lavish do. The bride, looking trim and triumphant, wore a smart, tailor-made costume. Toasts were drunk. There was no shortage of liquor. And there was tea, coffee, cakes and sandwiches in abundance. Over-abundance, in fact, calling forth from the bride a 'joke' which, later, would be held in sinister evidence against her. To a guest's polite observation regarding the overwhelming plenitude of the reception's provisions, the new Mrs Wilson cracked, 'We'll just save them for the funeral.' Then added, 'Although I might give this one a week's extension!'

She changed her mind.

Mr Wilson lived just thirteen days.

Back at the bungalow, the celebrations well past, poor Ernest was now securely in the hinged clasp of the preying black widow, to be, like some kinds of male spider, eaten after (or in his case, one suspects, without) the nuptial dance. As in the case of the late Oliver Leonard, Mrs Wilson took the precautionary step of involving a doctor *before* administering the *coup mortel*. With a cunning born of loving practice, she persuaded the unsuspecting Ernest that he had upset his stomach by eating too much liver for supper. She told him to stay in bed and she would get the doctor to look in and give him something that would soon put him right. When Dr Wallace came, old Ernest told him that he was not ill. The doctor nodded as he scribbled a prescription. But Mrs Wilson's objective had been achieved. She had

44

implanted in the doctor's head the notion that old Mr Wilson was ailing.

Late on the Monday night – 11 November 1957 – Mary called at the nearby house of her friend, Mrs Grace Liddell, also a widow. She told her that her new husband had been taken into hospital suddenly and she didn't fancy staying in the bungalow on her own. Mrs Liddell said that she would put her up for the night.

On the Tuesday morning, Mrs Liddell saw Mrs Wilson back to her bungalow. As they walked up the garden path, Mary handed her friend the keys to open the front door. 'You're going to get a shock,' she said.

Mrs Liddell unlocked the door and stepped inside. She had just time to register the fact that the house was in a filthy condition before recoiling from her predicted shock. There was Ernest – stone-white, marble-cold dead – laid out on a trestle, ready for burial.

She turned to Mary. It was almost an automatic reaction. 'Have you done anything to Ernest?' she asked.

'Don't be silly,' said the Widow Wilson.

Dr Wallace was not too surprised when he got the call telling him that old Ernest Wilson was dead. He was good as gold about issuing a death certificate – cardiac muscular failure.

If Ernest's death less than a fortnight after his wedding had not aroused suspicion, the Widow Wilson's subsequent behaviour would certainly have done so. To the undertaker who came to measure him for his coffin, she suggested – half arch humour, half avid intent – that, as she had given him so much business, he might give her a wholesale price. Shades again of Seddon and Smith. The old theory that the murderer *wants* to be caught seems well supported by the quite extraordinary conduct of the bereaved Mary Wilson. And, indeed, official interest had by now been engaged. The pace at which she was losing husbands savoured, as Lady Bracknell might have said, of criminal carelessness. Less elegantly, one of the local detectives put it like this: 'She certainly seemed hell-bent on getting rid of them – as though she was working against the clock.'

But what baffled the police when they first began their enquiries was the question of motive. Surely the paltry gleanings from these deaths could not be an inducement to murder. They were still privately inclined to put the deaths down to coincidence. Such things *do* happen. But as the rumours multiplied and stray reports of suspicious behaviour came to their knowledge, the police decided to take such action as would indicate one way or the other what credence they should give to local gossip and feeling. They applied for, and were granted, permission to exhume the Widow Wilson's last two spouses.

Those exhumations were carried out under conditions of great secrecy on 30 November 1957. While the general practitioners who had attended the dead men had had no reason to think that the deaths were anything other than natural, a disquietingly different state of affairs was revealed when the specialists, the pathologists, took over and unpicked the bodies at the seams. Plying scalpel, microscope and test-tube, they found that neither Wilson nor Leonard had died naturally. The post-mortem showed that Wilson had no serious organic disease, and that Leonard's heart was normal and there was no sign of chronic nephritis. What was found was, in Wilson's case, congestion in the oesophagus and intestines, and that the liver, instead of presenting the normal sort of chocolate brownish colour, was yellow. What was found in both bodies was elemental phosphorus, a deadly poison, in sufficient quantity to kill.

Aware after the exhumations of the growing climate of suspicion that she had made away with two of her husbands, the Widow Wilson is reported to have said: 'I know what people are saying. They think I murdered them. They say I murdered them to get money for drink. That's rubbish. I know I upset some people by that joke at my wedding, but I think that really people are jealous of me because I have always tried to laugh my way through life. I've had plenty of troubles, but

46

I believe in keeping cheerful. My conscience is clear. I have looked after all my men as a good wife should. Who knows? I might marry again if the right man comes along. I refuse to let gossips ruin my life.' Then, after another bit of reckless gallows-humour, 'I didn't kill them. They were dead already!' the incautious Mary sped busily off to spend the rest of her last day of liberty trying to sell Ernest's gold-plated watch and chain.

Mrs Wilson seemed genuinely surprised when the police called on her shortly after the resurrections of Oliver and Ernest, and began asking some extremely deep-digging questions. She did her not-very-successful best to provide some answers. The police, unconvinced, thereupon invited her to come on down to the station, where in due course they charged her with the murders of both men.

Her day of judgment had come.

Mary Elizabeth Wilson, the much-widowed, took her place before her earthly judges.

Leeds Assizes. March 1958.

On the bench: Mr Justice Hinchcliffe (his first murder trial).

Leading for the Crown: Mr Geoffrey Veale, QC.

Leading for the Defence: Miss Rose Heilbron, QC.

A jury constituted of nine men and three women.

The case was unusual in several respects. The prisoner was the first person to be tried simultaneously for two murders since the passing of the new Homicide Act 1957, under which hanging was generally abolished. The allegation that she had murdered her last two husbands on different occasions, if proved against her, would make the crime a capital one – for which, on conviction, she could only be sentenced to death. Clearly, Miss Heilbron would – and did at the start of the trial, in the absence of the jury – make a submission for separate trials. It was refused. The prosecution's claim that they were entitled to look from the facts of one case to those of the other for the purpose of considering whether what had happened was an accident, or an

47

evidenced 'system', as in the George Joseph Smith brides-in-the-bath case, succeeded. Unusual also was the circumstance that whereas it was the custom of either the Attorney General or the Solicitor General to prosecute in person in a poison trial, in this case the practice was not followed. Geoffrey Veale had recently succeeded Hinchcliffe as Recorder of Leeds.

Mr Veale rose and opened the prosecution's case. He described Mrs Wilson as a wicked woman who had, in succession, married two men and then deliberately poisoned them in order to receive their money and possessions. In the examinations which followed the exhumations of Leonard and Wilson, there was exhibited the indisputable presence of elemental phosphorus, a deadly poison. There was also found in Wilson's stomach a quantity of wheat bran. Rat poison and beetle poison are made up of a mixture of phosphorus, wheat bran and syrup.

'If you get phosphorus and wheat bran in somebody's stomach, can it,' Mr Veale asked, 'lead to any other conclusion but that that person has taken either rat or beetle poison?'

He proceeded to outline to the jury the story of the prisoner's meeting with Oliver Leonard, her enquiries as to his financial standing, her seduction of him as a lodger, and subsequent marriage to him. 'It may be you will come to the conclusion that the accused tried at once to get hold of such money as Leonard had. Leonard died two days after he had seen a doctor, who had thought that he was in good health for his age, and had given him a bottle of cough mixture.'

We come now to Mr Wilson. On 11 November 1957, a Dr Wallace visited Wilson. He had been sent for by Mrs Wilson. She told him that her husband had been bad through the night, but Wilson apparently did not complain. Dr Wallace thought there was some degeneration of the heart muscle, and gave him some tablets and a cough mixture, but he did not consider that there was anything alarming about his condition. The next day the doctor received an urgent telephone call telling him that Wilson was ill or dying. He went at once, and found Wilson dead.

'Another case,' Veale pointed out, 'where no doctor saw the victim shortly before death.' That night of 11 November, Mrs Wilson went to stay with a Mrs Liddell, and told her that her husband was bad and was always wanting water. 'Notice that observation. You will hear that an intense thirst is one of the symptoms of phosphorus poisoning.'

Veale said that, three days after the funeral, Mrs Wilson drew sums of £9 4s 11d. and £15 13s 4d. on two insurance policies. There was one piece of evidence which he thought that the jury might feel to be significant. It was the fact that no tin or container of rat or beetle poison was found. If it had been a case in either instance of accident or suicide, the container would have been there.

Mrs Alice Mary Connelly testified that it was while Mr Leonard was a lodger with her and her husband that he had been introduced to Mrs Wilson – or, rather, Mrs Knowles, as she was then. Mrs Knowles had asked if she could speak with him, and was with him for twenty minutes. The next day she announced, 'We're going to get married. He'll be leaving you.'

Cross-examined by Miss Heilbron, Mrs Connelly agreed that, because of Mrs Knowles, she was losing a good lodger, but denied that she was upset, because, she said, she felt that the couple would be happy.

Dr John Hubert Laydon went into the witness box. He stated that he had seen Mr Leonard on Monday, 1 October 1956. He was at that time a perfectly healthy man for his age. There was some bronchitis and a degree of arterial trouble, but he was not making much of his ailments. Dr Laydon said that he certainly did not suspect poisoning when he saw Leonard that day. He was not, however, surprised when he heard of his death, and had filled in a death certificate without actually seeing the body.

Miss Heilbron asked how he knew that Leonard was dead.

He replied, 'Some person came in and told me Mr Leonard was dead and I filled in the death certificate.'

'How did you fill in the blank, the gap between when you saw him and a week later?' asked Miss Heilbron.

'It wasn't a week. It was two days later. The man's condition is not going to change in two days. My examination on the first warranted his sudden death on the third.'

Dr Laydon added that a doctor was permitted to issue a death certificate without seeing the body if he had seen the person within fourteen days of the death. He felt fully justified in giving the death certificate.

Turning now to the case of Ernest Wilson, Mrs Grace Marion Liddell told how, on 11 November 1957, she was in bed when Mrs Wilson called on her and asked if she could stay the night. She had said that she could, and she did. Mrs Liddell recounted how, the next morning, she had gone with Mrs Wilson to the bungalow in Rectory Road. 'She told me I would get a shock when I went in. I went in and I did get a shock.' Mr Wilson's corpse was laid out on a trestle 'with a white thing over his face. I took the white thing off and kissed him.' The witness added that the bungalow was in a dreadful state – 'worse than a dog kennel.'

Dr William Proudfoot Wallace told the court that he had been sent for by Mrs Wilson on 11 November 1957. When he arrived at the bungalow, Mrs Wilson told him that her husband had been ill all night. He found Mr Wilson sitting up in bed. He was quite cheerful. The doctor said that he came to the conclusion that Wilson was suffering from myocardial degeneration. He prescribed a cough mixture and some tablets, in neither of which there was any phosphorus, and decided to call and see Wilson again in three days' time. However, on the morning of 12 November, he had received a call from the telephone box telling him that Wilson was very ill. He went at once and found that he was dead.

Now it was the turn of the pathologists and forensic scientists.

First, Dr William Stewart, who performed the post-mortem on the disinterred body of Ernest Wilson. Dr Stewart did not think that death was due to natural causes, but was the resul. of poisoning.

Miss Heilbron asked him, the inflection of her voice underlining for the jury's benefit the import of her question, 'These cases of Wilson and Leonard were the first cases of phosphorus poisoning you have done in your life?'

'Yes.'

Dr Ian Barclay, of the Forensic Science Laboratory, Gosforth, replying to Miss Heilbron, said that, outside chemical laboratories, the only other source of elemental phosphorus which he knew of was in rat and beetle poison.

'Do you know it is found in a pill?' asked Miss Heilbron.

'Maybe.'

'Do you know yellow phosphorus pills are on the lists of five well-known manufacturing chemists?'

'No.'

'You never enquired?'

'No.'

'Have you ever heard of damiana pills being used as an aphrodisiac?'

'I have never heard of that.'

The counsel for the defence said that she would be producing a box of those pills bought that morning.

Clearly the defence line was that Messrs Leonard and Wilson had both reacted to the (well) hidden charms of their new bride by fortifying their flagging libidos with doses of uplifting damiana.

In reply to further questions, Dr Barclay agreed that it was usual to keep elemental phosphorus submerged in water because it was unstable, anxious to pick up oxygen and reach a stable or oxidised state.

51

Miss Heilbron: 'Have you heard of many cases where phosphorus has been found in a body after as long as thirteen months?'

Dr Barclay: 'To the best of my knowledge there is no previously recorded case of phosphorus being recovered after as long as that. I know of no other case longer than six months.'

'Is it not, therefore, surprising, as this is the first recorded case, to find phosphorus in a body so long after?'

'I don't think it is surprising, for the reason that phosphorus can be protected by the fatty material and its free state preserved. It might be described as being sealed up in the fat.'

Counsel leapt in, very quick off the mark: 'Yet the organ that we know was fatty – the liver – was one in which you found so little phosphorus that you could not quantify it?'

'Yes, but the amounts which eventually arrive in that organ are so small they are of microgram quantity, about one-millionth of a gram per cent of tissue.'

With regard to the amount of elemental phosphorus constituting a fatal dose, Dr Barclay said, 'You must take a fair amount to make sure that a small proportion gets to work.'

One grain is equivalent to 64.5 milligrams. So, a fatal dose of 1½ grains would be about 100 milligrams.

Dr Barclay explained that there were two types of yellow phosphorus poisoning. In the first, where there was ingestion of an apparently large amount, death ensued fairly rapidly. In the second, where the amount ingested was much smaller, there were mild symptoms for one or two days; for another two or three days the person seemed to be back to normal, and then suddenly, on the fifth, sixth or seventh day, death took place. It was in this second type that jaundice became apparent. The cases of both Leonard and Wilson belonged to the first type, death occuring in the first phase, comparatively quickly.

Dr David Ernest Price, a pathologist, also thought that both men had died in the first stage of phosphorus poisoning. In reply to Miss Heilbron's question as to whether it was right that there was no scientific method of assessing the amount of phosphorus ingested in a body after two weeks because no one knew the rate of oxidisation, he said, 'All I can say is that I recovered yellow phosphorus indicative of the consumption of a relatively large dose.'

Dr Alan Stewart Currie, Scientific Officer of the Home Office Laboratory, Harrogate, deposed that he had received from Dr Barclay specimens for analysis to see if he could find in them any poison or drug other than phosphorus. He found none. Purely for his own interest, he tested also for elemental phosphorus. That test yielded positive results.

Miss Heilbron asked whether he had ever heard of elemental phosphorus being used in pills. 'The French,' he said, 'used it at the beginning of this century. There have been many strange things used in pills. I have never come across elemental phosphorus used in pills, but it did have some use at the beginning of the century. I read the other day that phosphorus has no place in modern clinical medicine.'

Miss Heilbron handed a small bottle to Dr Currie. 'Look at this bottle of damiana pills.'

'May I break one?' Dr Currie took a pill from the bottle and crushed it with a coin on the ledge of the witness box, then scooped the fragments into the palm of his hand and sniffed them. 'Yes,' he said. 'There is a little phosphorus there – at least the smell of it.'

'Do you know that that pill is used, or can be used, as an aphrodisiac?'

'No, I don't. It is said to be in the *British Pharmacopoeia* of 1934.'

'Yes, but I am producing this bottle in 1958,' said Counsel. She then referred to *The American Illustrated Medical Dictionary* (Dorland), 1951 edition, and quoted it as saying that phosphorus could be used for rickets, nervous and cerebral disease, and as a genital stimulant in sexual exhaustion.

Dr Currie's reaction to this information was, 'That's an amazing assortment. I don't think it would affect those things.' He also said that he doubted that, unless a very large amount of pills had been taken, phosphorus would be found in the body. It was the exception rather than the rule to isolate phosphorus – 'I have isolated it before, but you are very lucky to get it.'

Miss Heilbron called William Dixon, a former Newcastle CID sergeant, now employed as a private detective. He testified that, on the instructions of Mrs Wilson's solicitors, he had made enquiries to see if he could obtain damiana pills. He visited three wholesalers in Newcastle and each had a stock. The bottle of pills which Counsel had shown to the court was handed to him, and Dixon said that he had bought them from the retail section of a Newcastle chemist. They were sold over the counter and no doctor's prescription was needed.

Mr Veale asked, 'Has the bottle got a label "Poison" on it in red?'

'Yes.'

Next came Mr Angus Fraser McIntosh, the manager of Rodine, the rat poison manufacturer. He spoke of examining pills bought at a Newcastle chemists. He said that each pill – there were fifty to the bottle – contained one-hundredth of a grain of elemental phosphorus; just short of a milligram. The amount of phosphorus found in Wilson's body was 2.7 milligrams, equal to five of the pills. In the case of Leonard, the 3.8 milligrams found was equal to six or seven pills. Pharmaceutically, the pills were an aphrodisiac for the treatment of sexual debility and to increase sexual desire. He understood that a fatal dose of phosphorus was $1\frac{1}{2}$ grains, so to obtain a fatal dose from the pills it would be necessary to swallow 150 of them.

Veale asked, 'To get a fatal dose you would have to take three whole bottles full?'

'That is right,' McIntosh replied.

Dr Francis Camps was called by the defence. He came into the case in the role of defendant's best friend, but he came as an expert outsider for he had not himself examined the bodies. His evidence would therefore be based on medical and scientific reports. He had, however, one great advantage over most of the other doctors involved. He had actually seen several cases of phosphorus poisoning. He agreed that treatment was available, and that that treatment was better given in hospital. Mrs Wilson had, of course, made no effort to get treatment for her husband.

Miss Heilbron asked Dr Camps what would be the respective causes of death in the first and second types of phosphorus poisoning. He replied that in the first it would be heart failure. In the second it would be liver failure, but there would also be renal failure, and the heart muscle and various other muscles would be affected.

A question of paramount importance to the defence was how, if she were guilty, Mrs Wilson had administered the phosphorus. Dr Camps said that in a previous case of phosphorus poisoning which he had investigated, in order to see how easy it was to take rat poison, various methods of administration were tested – such as in beer, cider and spirits, in tea, and on bread and blackcurrant jam. The last of these methods, it was found, would hide the taste and appearance, but, he added, he would expect to find evidence of the jam.

Miss Heilbron enquired, 'Can you administer Rodine as it is?'

'A person would have to be blind and without taste or smell. There is a cloud of vapour as soon as you open the tin. A strong odour. The taste is horrible.'

He further said that if Rodine was taken in jam, a great deal depended on the jam and the type of vehicle used with it. In a case of this sort, it was essential to examine the contents of the stomach, to find any foreign bodies and to see what kind of food had been taken. If the phosphorus had not been given in tea, there was a strong possibility that it was disguised in cough mixture. (Both men had similar bottles of it, and one of the bottles contained a teaspoonful of Rodine.)

Asked if he was prepared to give a cause of death, Dr Camps replied, 'The findings of the cause of death are pathologically contradictory. In view of the contradictory findings, and in the absence of microscopic evidence, I would not be prepared to say.' But if asked to *suggest* a cause of death, he would say that Wilson died from heart failure and Leonard from cerebral thrombosis. These were, however, only suggestions. 'If I were asked to put a cause of death, I would put "unascertainable".'

Further pressed, Dr Camps would not commit himself with regard to the cause of death in the case of Wilson, but he did not think that it must necessarily have been phosphorus poisoning. 'I think it would be dangerous to say that, because other causes of death have not been excluded.'

Miss Heilbron enquired, 'What other causes could there have been in an old man of seventy-six on the findings here?'

'The commonest cause of death at that age is undoubtedly heart condition.'

'Is diabetes a possibility?'

'No, I don't think it is a possible cause of death, but it is a possible cause of fatty changes in the liver. But there are lots of other things which might be a cause of change.'

In cross-examination, Mr Veale handed Camps a bottle. Camps sniffed it and said that it smelled like cough mixture.

'Would you,' asked Veale, 'be surprised that there is more than a teaspoonful of Rodine rat poison in that bottle?'

'Yes; that is, I believe, exactly what I said about disguise. This,' said Camps, holding the bottle to his nose again, 'is a very good disguise.'

In reply to further questions, Camps stated that he had been professionally involved in a number of phosphorus poisoning cases. He described what he called first- and second-stage cases. In the first stage, death occurred usually between six and ten hours, after sickness, pain, intense thirst and prostration. In second-stage cases, death took longer, causing changes in the liver.

He thought that if Leonard and Wilson had died of phosphorus poisoning, they were second-stage cases, because of the fatty changes that had taken place in their livers. He had seen the liver sections from both bodies. This was in direct contradiction of the opinion expressed by Dr Barclay.

Commenting on the evidence given by Dr William Stewart, who examined the bodies after the exhumations, Camps pointed out that Dr Stewart had said that he did not take sections of other parts of the bodies. He had thought they were unnecessary. Said Camps, 'No autopsy in any case of poison can be complete without full pathological examination of the adjoining organs.'

Veale asked Camps whether it was some form of coincidence that they were investigating the deaths of not one but two men who had something in the gullet, intestines and liver, and also had phosphorus in the stomach.

Camps' reply was, 'I don't think the gullet and liver have any significance. The only thing I would think of any significance, which could be interpreted, is phosphorus.'

'What about symptoms?' demanded Veale. 'We now have a pallor, pain, restlessness and mental change in Leonard's case.'

Camps: 'If that was put to a student in examination, he would not mention phosphorus poisoning in his diagnosis. It is only a picture of anyone dying.'

'You said Wilson died of heart failure, something that stopped his heart. What was it?' asked Veale.

'I don't know.'

'But might not phosphorus poisoning have stopped Wilson's heart?'

'It could have done. The only thing that worries me is that there are, in my view, too many things missing.'

'You have not had the advantage of being present at the post-mortems?'

'No.'

'Of seeing the actual livers?'

'I saw what remained of them.'

57

Dr Camps was cautious when his attention was called to the opinion expressed by Dr Price that the deaths were due to phosphorus poisoning.

Veale suggested that Dr Price and Dr Stewart were right, and Dr Camps was wrong. Camps rejoined, 'I don't think Dr Price materially differs from me, from what I have heard. I have read the transcripts.'

'He says the cause of death was phosphorus poisoning. Do you agree?'

'I would not go as far as to say that.'

In her final address to the jury, Miss Heilbron explained why Mrs Wilson had not gone into the witness box to give evidence. 'She has given a very full and frank statement to the police. She has said the deaths are a mystery, and she certainly cannot assist you on the scientific side. Don't hold it against her, because she has accepted my advice.'

This brought instant and sharp rebuke from the judge. 'The jury do not want to know what advice you gave to the prisoner. You know you should not have said it.'

Counsel, having made her point, made her apologies. 'I am sorry, my lord.'

Referring to the evidence given by the prosecution's scientific witnesses, Miss Heilbron said, 'They are all human, all fallible, and all can make mistakes.' She said that one invariable symptom of phosphorus poisoning was vomiting. In neither case had the prosecution produced any evidence that vomiting had occurred.

Dealing with Dr Stewart's testimony that in each case there was fatty degeneration of the liver as a result of phosphorus poisoning, she suggested that the post-mortem examinations left much to be desired. Dr Stewart had said that the heart muscle was perfectly healthy and that he did not make a microscopic examination because he could see that much with the naked eye. 'Is this tremendous artifice of science, the microscope, not to be used to discover all the facts?' she demanded.

Counsel made great play with the fact that in neither instance had the death certificate given the true cause of death, and that neither of the bodies had been seen after death by the family doctor – although this was actually quite a common practice where nothing other than natural causes was suspected.

Regarding the damiana pills, Counsel said that she had introduced them in order to show an alternative method of obtaining phosphorus. 'What more natural than that these old men, finding a wife in the evening of their lives, should purchase these pills for the purpose for which they are apparently known? . . . Is it not another coincidence in this woman's favour? Bear in mind the agony of this old woman and the phrase she used when one of her husbands died, 'I'm lonely now he's gone.' There is no evidence that Mrs Wilson had possessed phosphorus. This woman has gone through a heavy ordeal and a terrible agony. Do you think the evidence proves she is the diabolical poisoner she is said to be? I ask you to say she is not guilty.'

No one could have been defended more ably.

Addressing the jury on behalf of the Crown, Mr Veale said that the issues were not complicated, but as simple and plain as a pikestaff. Phosphorus was not something to be taken by accident. What, he asked, was the relevance of pills introduced by the defence – pills containing microscopic quantities of phosphorus? A fatal dose was about 150 pills. They were supplied in shops in small bottles. But were any small pill bottles found in the houses of Leonard and Wilson? Wouldn't they have been found if these pills had been bought? The jury might feel that any complications in the case had been introduced by the defence in an attempt to blur their vision.

'This,' said Veale, 'is a case of deliberate poisoning. What is the alternative? Suicide does not seem to be suggested. Accident? An overdose of something? Of what? One hundred and fifty aphrodisiac pills in two cases? The answer is all too plain. It is no accident but deliberate poisoning.'

On the facts, it was obvious that the judge would sum up against Mrs Wilson. In his summing-up he paid very great attention to the medical and scientific evidence, and restated the symptoms of phosphorus poisoning as listed by the experts.

'Who,' asked Mr Justice Hinchcliffe, 'is the only living person today who can tell what were the symptoms from which Leonard and Wilson suffered? Why is it that she has not been called to give evidence on oath on these important matters? The prosecution's case is that it is established beyond doubt that Leonard and Wilson died from phosphorus poisoning. If you accept that these men died from phosphorus poisoning, you will ask yourselves how did these two old men come to take and ingest phosphorus? Has Mrs Wilson – it is a rhetorical question – helped you all she could? She has chosen not to give evidence on oath, so you are without her explanation on many important matters.' These included the details and lengths of her husbands' illnesses; the reason why a doctor was not called in each case; her odd behaviour with Mrs Liddell on the day after Wilson's death; her trying to sell a watch and chain a few days later; her alleged queer and untrue statement that her husband was ill in hospital, when he was in fact lying dead at home. These lies and actions had all to be considered.

Pills containing phosphorus had been produced and the suggestion had been made that two men in their mid-seventies had taken them as sexual stimulants. The jury should, said the judge, give that suggestion as much weight as it deserved. You have had no evidence called before you that either Leonard or Wilson ever possessed one of these bottles of pills.'

Dr Camps had expressed the view, in evidence, that bran found in the intestines of both men was the same sort as in brown bread. 'But there is no evidence that brown bread was eaten in either the Leonard or Wilson household. Dr Camps is not prepared to say what was the cause of death. He agrees that phosphorus was found, and Dr Barclay agrees with Dr Price in confirming that there was no other poison in the bodies.'

Because he had had to give evidence in a case at Lewes Assizes, Dr Camps had arrived a day late at Leeds and, perhaps, created the unfortunate, and completely unfair, impression that 'the man from the South' was slighting a northern court. Camps was the first to admit that his evidence, while positively for the defence, was full of suppositions and theories. He made no other claim. Even so, he was finally somewhat humiliated by the judge, who, apparently ignoring Camps' superior status as a consultant specialist, instructed the jury that they must give his evidence only the same weight as that of any of the other and several medico-legal witnesses.

The defence had asked the jury to take the view that the post-mortem examinations conducted by Dr Stewart left much to be desired, should have been carried out with greater caution, and that more microscopic sections of various parts of the bodies should have been taken. 'You will pay such attention to these criticisms as they deserve. Dr Stewart, a doctor of medicine, a distinguished pathologist, a professional man, gave independent evidence, with a view to assisting the court to come to the right conclusion.'

The jury, after an absence of an hour and twenty-five minutes, found Mrs Wilson guilty of both murders. She was the first person to be convicted and sentenced for more than one murder under the new Homicide Act, and the first woman to be sentenced to death under it.

She heard the death sentence unmoved.

As it turned out, she was not hanged. After the appeal had been dismissed, the Home Secretary granted her a reprieve. No official reason was given. It is possible that her age – sixty-six – was a factor. In his excellent book, *Reprieve: A Study of a System* (1965), Fenton Bresler hazards that it is more likely that she was reprieved 'primarily because she was a woman, because, possibly among other reasons, Lord Butler, then Home Secretary, could not bring himself to order her execution, complete with the ritual donning of rubber knickers'.

It is reported that, five days after she arrived at Holloway to start a life sentence, inquests were held on John Knowles and John George Russell – husband and lover. Dr Stewart, who twice again obliged with knife, tube and microscope, came up with another phosphorus double. Detective Chief Inspector Mitchell, finding himself unable to produce any court-worthy evidence as to how the life-destroying phosphorus came to be in the bodies, had to stand frustratedly by as open verdicts were formally recorded.

For the much-marrying Widow of Windy Nook, harbinger of death to so many grooms, Death himself was her last bridegroom. He came to claim her in 1962, behind the bars of the prison she had, by her actions, freely made for herself. The constant bride was aged seventy when she succumbed to the final groom's embrace.

# The Medea of Kew Gardens Hills
## Albert Borowitz

On the morning of 14 July 1965, Eddie Crimmins received a telephone call from his estranged wife Alice, accusing him of having taken the children. When she had opened their bedroom door, which she kept locked by a hook-and-eye on the outside, she had seen that the beds had been slept in but Eddie Jr, aged five, and his four-year-old sister Alice (nicknamed Missy) were gone. The casement window was cranked open about 75 degrees; Alice remembered having closed it the night before because there was a hole in the screen and she wanted to keep the bugs out. The screen was later found outside, leaning against the wall beneath the window, and nearby was a 'porter's stroller' – a converted baby-carriage with a box on it.

Alice's husband, an aeroplane mechanic who worked nights, protested that he knew nothing of the children's whereabouts and, alarmed by the message, said he would come right over to see her. Alice and the children lived in a dispiriting redbrick apartment complex flatteringly named Regal Gardens, located near the campus of Queens College in the Kew Gardens Hills section of the New York City borough of Queens. Shortly after joining his wife, Eddie called the police, and the first contingent of patrolmen were on the scene in a matter of minutes. By 11 a.m. precinct cars were parked all around the grassy mall adjoining Alice's apartment building at 150–22 72nd Drive.

Jerry Piering, who was the first detective to arrive,

quickly made the case his own. Hoping for a promotion to second grade on the Queens' detective command, he immediately sensed that he had stepped into an important investigation. It took only one glance at Alice for him to decide that she did not look the picture of the anxious mother, this striking redhead in her twenties, with thick make-up, hip-hugging toreador slacks, flowered blouse and white high-heeled shoes. Patrolman Michael Clifford had already filled Piering in on the background – the Crimminses were separated and in the middle of a custody fight, but the role that the vanished children might have played in their skirmishing was still obscure.

The first fruits of Piering's look around the premises confirmed the unfavourable impression Alice had made. In the garbage cans there were about a dozen empty liquor bottles that Alice later attributed to good house-keeping rather than over-indulgence, explaining that she had been cleaning the apartment in anticipation of an inspection visit from a city agency in connection with the custody suit. Still more revealing to Piering was a proverbial 'little black book' that Alice had dropped outside; the men listed outnumbered women four to one. While Piering was making his rounds, Detective George Martin found trophies of Alice's active social life in a pastel-coloured overnight bag stowed under her bed. The greetings and dinner programmes that filled the bag documented her relationship with Anthony (Tony) Grace, a fifty-two-year-old highway contractor with ties to important Democratic politicians. Alice's souvenirs showed that Tony Grace had introduced her to such party stalwarts as Mayor Robert Wagner and Senator Robert Kennedy; messages from Grace and important city officials addressed her as 'Rusty'.

Piering took Alice into her bedroom and questioned her about her activities on 13 July. Between 2.30 and 4.30 in the afternoon she and the children had picnicked in Kissena Park, six blocks from the apartment. They came home after stopping to pick up some food for dinner; at Sever's delicatessen in the neighbourhood she had bought a package of frozen veal, a can of string beans and a bottle of soda. When she arrived home she called her attorney, Michael LaPenna (recommended to her by Grace), to discuss the custody case which was scheduled for a hearing in a week. She was concerned about a former maid, Evelyn Linder Atkins, who claimed that Alice owed her $600 and, according to Alice, had hinted that if she were paid she would not testify against her in the proceedings. Evelyn had a worrisome story to tell the judge if she decided to do so, for Alice had without warning abandoned the children one weekend while she took a boat trip to the Bahamas with Tony Grace and his friends. Alice told Piering that it was not her fault; she had thought she was aboard only for a *bon voyage* party but the men had playfully locked her and a girlfriend in a washroom and carried them off to sea. Perhaps LaPenna shared her concern about the maid, because the lawyer did not seem as optimistic about her chances of retaining custody as he usually did.

After dinner, Alice took the children for a ride in the direction of Main Street, wanting to find out the location of a furnished apartment to which her husband had recently moved. Knowing that Eddie had planted a crude 'bug' on her telephone, she was hoping to retaliate by finding him to be living with a woman. She drove around for more than an hour until it was almost dark and then gave up the search.

Upon returning home, Alice prepared the children for bed about 9 p.m. (Theresa Costello, aged fourteen, Alice's former babysitter, later told the police that it was at this very moment that, passing below the bedroom window on her way to a babysitting job, she heard the Crimmins children saying their prayers.) Alice brought a replacement screen from her room to the children's bedroom but noticed that it had been fouled by her dog, Brandy. She therefore reset the children's punctured screen in the window without bothering to bolt it into place. Mindful of the coming agency visit, she disposed of wine and liquor bottles and made a pile of old clothing; by 10.30 p.m. she was tired, and collapsed on the living-room couch to watch *The Defenders* on TV. The programme did not make her forget that Tony Grace had not returned the call she had made earlier in the day. She reached him at a Bronx bar and to her jealous questions he responded that he was alone. After she hung up, Alice received a call from a man Grace had apparently replaced in her favour, a house renovator named Joe Rorech. Alice had met Rorech in January 1964 when she was working as a cocktail waitress at the Bourbon House in Syosset, Long Island. After Eddie had moved out of the Crimmins apartment, another Bourbon House waitress, Anita ('Tiger') Ellis, had come to live with Alice. For a while they had shared the favours of Joe Rorech, but 'Tiger' had soon moved on to new attachments. In their conversation last night, Joe Rorech asked Alice to join him at a bar in Huntington, Long Island, but she evaded the invitation pleading the unavailability of a babysitter.

After talking to Joe, Alice returned to her television set. At midnight she took little Eddie to the bathroom but could not wake Missy; she thought she had re-latched the bedroom door. (The door was kept locked, she explained, to keep Eddie from raiding the refrigerator.) Afterwards, Alice took the dog Brandy for a walk, then sat on the front stoop for a while. She told Piering that she may not have bolted the front door at the time. When at last she was getting ready for bed, her husband called and angered her by repeating the maid's claim that Alice owed her money. Alice calmed down by taking the dog out again and, after a bath, went to sleep between 3.30 and 4 a.m.

Alice and Eddie, childhood sweethearts, had been married seven years. They were reasonably happy for a while but, soon after the birth of their son, they quarrelled frequently about Eddie's staying out late working or drinking with friends. After Missy was born, Alice decided to have no more children and Eddie, brought up a good Catholic (as was she) never forgave her after he found birth control devices in her purse. Their relationship went from bad to worse until, on 22 June 1965, he went to the Family Court to seek custody of the two children. By then, the couple were already separated, the children living on with Alice at the Regal Gardens.

66

The custody petition charged that, immediately after the separation, Alice 'began to indulge herself openly and brazenly in sex as she had done furtively before the separation'. It was further detailed in the petition that Alice 'entertains, one at a time, a stream of men sharing herself and her bedroom, until she and her paramour of the evening are completely spent. The following morning, the children awake to see a strange man in the house.'

Combining a high degree of jealousy with a flair for the technology of snooping, Eddie had devoted many of his leisure hours to surveillance of her relations with men. He had much to observe, for when Alice gave up her secretarial work to become a waitress at a series of Long Island restaurants and bars, her opportunities for male acquaintance multiplied. To keep his compulsive watch, Eddie bugged her telephone and installed a microphone in her bedroom which he could monitor from a listening-post he had established in the basement below. Once he had burst in on Alice and a usually overdressed waiter named Carl Andrade, who had fled naked out of the window to his car.

Eddie liked to think that the purpose of his spying was to gather evidence for the custody case, but he ultimately admitted that he had often invaded Alice's apartment when she was out just to be near her 'personal things'. During their separation, so Alice said, Eddie told her that he had exposed himself to little girls in a park, but Alice disbelieved him, thinking that he was trying to play on her sympathy for his loneliness and distress.

Eddie's preoccupation with his wife's love life dominated his activities on 13 July, as he recounted them to the police. At 7 a.m. he had played a poor round of golf at a public course at Bethpage in Nassau County. Afterwards he drank three beers in the clubhouse with a friend and watched the New York Mets baseball game on television, leaving around 2 p.m. before the game ended. He then drove to Huntington to see whether Alice was visiting Joe Rorech but was disappointed to find no sign of her four-year-old Mercury convertible there. He arrived home at 5 p.m. and spent the evening watching television.

Then, about 11 p.m., he drove along Union Turnpike to a small fast food stand near St John's University, bought a pizza and a large bottle of Pepsi Cola, and returned home. Alice, though, was still very much on his mind. After driving back to the Union Turnpike and drinking gin and tonic at a bar until 2.45 a.m., he drove into the parking lot behind his wife's bedroom window; he thought he saw a light there and in her living-room. He went home and called up Alice to talk about the maid. When Alice hung up, he watched a movie on television, read briefly and fell asleep by 4 a.m. A detective who checked out Eddie's story found that the movie he claimed to have seen on the CBS channel had actually been on much earlier.

In addition to questioning Alice, Jerry Piering, a fledgling in his job, directed the police inspection and photographing of the apartment, apparently with more enthusiasm than expertise. Piering later claimed that when he first came into the children's room, he observed a thin layer of dust on the bureau-top, which in his mind eliminated the possibility that the children had left the room through the window since they would have had to cross over the bureau. However, technicians had covered the top of the bureau with powder for detecting fingerprints before the bureau could be photographed in its original condition. It was Piering's further recollection that when he had moved a lamp on the bureau, it had left a circle in the layer of dust. This story was later disputed by Alice's brother, John Burke, and others, who agreed that the lamp on the bureau had tripod legs. Also, many people had come into the room before Piering arrived; Eddie Crimmins had leaned out of the window to look for the missing children, and, of course, Alice on the previous evening had removed and replaced the screen; it seemed unlikely that Piering's dust-film would have remained undisturbed amid all this activity. In any event, neither the layer of dust nor the impression left by the lamp base was noted in Piering's first reports.

In the early afternoon of 14 July 1965, the Crimmins case was transformed from mysterious disappearance into homicide. A nine-year-old boy, Jay Silverman, found

Missy's body in an open lot on 162nd Street, about eight blocks from the Regal Gardens. A pyjama-top, knotted into two ligatures, was loosely tied around her bruised neck. An autopsy, performed with the participation of Dr Milton Helpern, New York City's distinguished Chief Medical Examiner, found no evidence of sexual assault; haemorrhages in the mucous membranes in the throat and vocal cords confirmed that Missy had been asphyxiated. The contents of the stomach were sent to an expert, who reported finding, among other things, a macaroni-like substance. This discovery rang a bell with Detective Piering, who recalled that on the morning of 14 July he had seen in Alice's trash can a package that had held frozen manicotti and had also noticed a plate of leftover manicotti in her refrigerator. However, none of this evidence had been preserved – nor had Piering's discoveries been referred to in his contemporaneous reports.

Following the discovery of Missy's body, the search for young Eddie intensified. A false alarm was raised in Cunningham Park when what looked like a blond-headed body turned out to be a discarded doll. On Monday morning, 19 July, Vernon Warnecke and his son, walking together to look at a treehouse used by the children in the neighbourhood, found Eddie Crimmins on an embankment overlooking the Van Wyck Expressway. The boy's body was eaten away by rats and insects and in an advanced state of decay. The site was about a mile from Alice Crimmins's apartment and close to the grounds of the New York World's Fair that was then in progress.

After the children were buried, Alice and her husband, reunited by their tragedy, faced a relentless police investigation which explored many trails, always only to return to Alice. Detectives pursued reports of strange intruders in the Crimmins neighbourhood, including a so-called 'pants burglar' who broke into homes only to steal men's trousers. A closer look was taken at the boyfriends whose names filled Alice's black book. Anthony Grace admitted in a second interview that he had lied when he told the police he had never left the Bronx on the night of 13/14 July. He now stated that he had driven over the Whitestone Bridge to a restaurant called Ripples on the Water with a group of 'bowling girls', young married women who partied around town under the pretext that they were going bowling. Grace maintained that he had stayed away from Alice during the period of the custody battle and had not seen her much recently. She had called him several times on 13 July but he was preoccupied with business and had taken his wife to dinner without remembering to call Alice back. At 11 p.m. she phoned him again at the Capri Bar, telling him that she wanted to join him for a drink. He had put her off by telling her that he was about to leave and had denied her well-founded suspicion that he was with the bowling girls.

Joe Rorech told Detective Phil Brady that he had called Alice twice on the night of the disappearance, first after 10 p.m., when she declined his invitation to the Bourbon House bar, and then at 2 a.m., when there had been no answer. Rorech had been drinking all night and admitted he might have misdialled the number. On 6 December 1965 the police administered the first of two sodium pentothal 'truth tests' to Rorech. Satisfied with the results, and finding Rorech's self-confidence weakened by business reverses, they conscripted him as a spy. Joe took Alice to motel rooms where recorders had been planted, but their conversations contained nothing of interest.

At first Eddie Crimmins had been more inclined to cooperate with the police than Alice. He submitted to a session with the lie detector, and persuaded Alice to take the test. However, after she agreed and the preliminary questions were completed, she refused to continue. With the exception of Detective Brady, the police now decided to forget about Eddie and concentrate on Alice. Before the Crimminses moved into a new three-room apartment in Queens to avoid the eyes of their unwanted public, the police, succeeding to the role long played by Alice's jealous husband, planted ultrasensitive microphones and tapped the telephone wires. Detectives monitored the apartment around the clock from the third floor pharmacy of a neighbouring hospital, but could not pick up a single incriminating statement. Their failure was not remarkable since Alice seemed well aware of the police presence, beginning many of her conversations, 'Drop dead, you guys!' Unable to overhear a confession, the secret listeners were tuned into the sounds of Alice's sexual encounters, which resumed shortly after she took up her new residence. As their high-tech recording devices picked up Alice's cries of physical need, her pursuers became more certain of her guilt, convinced as they were that grief for the dead children would demand an adjournment of the flesh.

According to reporter Kenneth Gross, who has written the principal account of the case, police investigators vented their hostility against Alice by interfering with the love affairs that they were recording so assiduously. When the tireless eaves-droppers overheard Joe Rorech and Alice making love, they informed Eddie Crimmins, who promptly called and was assured by Alice that she was alone. The police, hoping for a confrontation between lover and outraged husband, flattened Rorech's tyres, but he managed to have his car towed safely out of the neighbourhood before Eddie got home. When Alice moved out of the apartment to live with an Atlanta man for whom she was working as a secretary, the police thoughtfully advised the man's wife, and when she came to New York, helped her destroy Alice's clothing. Undaunted by this harassment, Alice reappeared in her familiar nightspots, now as a customer instead of cocktail waitress.

The investigation dragged on for a year and a half without result, and meanwhile there was a growing public clamour for action. At this point New York politics intervened to step up the pace of events: Nat Hentel, an interim Republican appointment as Queens District Attorney, was soundly defeated for re-election and decided to convene a grand jury before his term of office expired. The grand jury failed to return an indictment, and a second grand jury impanelled under Hentel's Democratic successor 'Tough Tommy' Mackell also disbanded without indictment in May of the following year. Then, on 1 September 1967, Assistant District Attorney James Mosley went before still another grand jury to present the testimony of a 'mystery witness', who was soon identified as Sophie Earomirski.

Sophie's original entrance into the case had been anonymous. On 30 November 1966, she had written to then District Attorney Hentel telling him how happy she was to read that he was bringing the Crimmins case to a grand jury. She reported an 'incident' she had witnessed while looking out of her living-room window on the early morning of 14 July 1965. Shortly after 2 a.m., a man and woman came walking down the street towards 72nd Road in Queens. The woman, who was lagging about five feet behind the man, was holding what appeared to be a bundle of blankets shining white under her left arm, and with her right hand led a little boy walking at her side. The man shouted at her to hurry up and she told him 'to be quiet or someone will see us'. The man took the blanket-like white bundle and heaved it onto the back seat of the nondescript automobile. The woman picked up the little boy and sat with him on the back seat; she had dark hair, and her companion was tall, not heavy, with dark hair and a large nose. Sophie apologised for signing merely as 'A Reader'.

Shortly after he was entrusted with the Crimmins case by Mackell, Mosley came across Sophie's letter, and the hunt for her began. The police obtained samples of the handwriting of tenants living in garden apartments from which the scene described in the letter could have been viewed, and they identified Sophie, who recognised Alice's photograph as resembling the woman she had seen. Sophie's testimony before the third grand jury was decisive, and Queens County finally had its long-coveted indictment, charging Alice Crimmins with the murder of Missy. The prosecution had persuaded the grand jury that there was reasonable cause to believe that the bundle of blankets Sophie had seen contained the little girl's dead body.

On 9 May 1968, the trial began in the ground floor

72

court-room of the Queens County Criminal Court Building amid widely varying perceptions of the defendant. To the sensationalist press, Alice was a 'modern-day Medea' who had sacrificed her children to a deadly hatred for her husband, and the pulp magazine *Front Page Detective*, invoking another witch from antiquity, called her an 'erring wife, a Circe, an amoral woman whose many affairs appeared symptomatic of America's Sex Revolution'. A group of radical feminists offered to identify Alice's cause with their own, but she declined their help. Between these two wings of public opinion there was a dominant vision of Alice as a manhunting cocktail waitress, and her longer years as housewife, mother and secretary receded into the background.

The prosecution case was presented for the most part by James Mosley's aspiring young assistant, Anthony Lombardino, but Mosley himself scored the first important point while questioning Dr Milton Helpern. The forensic expert testified that the discovery of as much food as was found in Missy's stomach was consistent with a post-ingestion period of less than two hours. If Helpern was right, then assuming that Alice had been the last to feed the children, she could not have seen them alive at midnight, as she claimed.

Lombardino insisted that the prize job of examining the prosecution's star witness was his – his alone. Since the police had first enlisted Joe Rorech's aid, Joe's difficulties had continued to mount; his marriage was in trouble and he had been upset by a brief period of arrest as a material witness. In his testimony he made it plain that he had lost any vestige of loyalty to his former mistress.

The defence, led by Harold Harrison, was unmoved when Rorech indirectly quoted Alice, 'She did not want Eddie to have the children. She would rather see the children dead than Eddie have them.' Harrison had not heard this before, but he did not regard the statement as damaging; surely the jury would understand that it was just the kind of thing that a divorcing spouse was likely to say in the heat of a custody battle. Rorech, though, had something more to disclose that would change the course of the trial. Though the police had learned nothing incriminating from electronic eavesdropping, Joe testified to a long conversation with Alice at a motel in Nassau County. After weeping inconsolably, she had said again and again that the children 'will understand, they know it was for the best'. At last she had added, 'Joseph, please forgive me, I killed her.'

Stung by the witness's words, Alice jumped out of her chair and banged her fists on the defence table, crying, 'Joseph! How could you do this? This is not true! Joseph . . . you, of all people! Oh, my God!' Harrison was unable to follow Alice's outburst with telling cross-examination for he had no effective means of rebutting Rorech's quotes. In fact, he may have been preoccupied by a dilemma of his own: the next morning he went before Judge Peter Farrell and unsuccessfully sought to withdraw from the case on the grounds that prior to the trial he had represented Joe Rorech as well as Alice, to whom Joe had introduced him.

After Rorech's damning testimony, the appearance of Sophie Earomirski, The Woman in the Window, came as an anticlimax. Sophie elaborated the scene she had recalled in her anonymous letter by adding a pregnant dog. She told the jury that the woman had responded to her male companion's order to hurry by explaining that she was waiting for the dog. She had said, 'The dog is pregnant,' and the man had grumbled, 'Did you have to bring it?' In fact, Brandy *was* pregnant that night, but several witnesses swore that nobody had recognised the pregnancy – that when the dog produced a single puppy the week after the killing, Alice and the neighbours were surprised.

The defence tried to destroy Sophie's credibility, but the scope of the attack was narrowly limited by Judge Farrell. The judge excluded an affidavit of Dr Louis Berg to the effect that a head injury suffered by Mrs Earomirski at the World's Fair had resulted in 'permanent brain damage'. Defence lawyer Marty Baron questioned her about two suicide attempts, but to no avail: the courtroom spectators cheered her recital that she had placed her head in an oven to see how dinner was coming along. A press photograph records Sophie's exit from the courthouse, her hand raised in triumph like a triumphant boxer, still champion, on whom the challenger could not lay a glove.

The principal strategy of the defence was to put Alice on the stand to deny the murder charge and to show that she was not made of granite, as portrayed by certain sections of the media. When Baron's questioning turned to the children, Alice began to tremble and whispered to Judge Farrell that she could not continue. Farrell declared a recess. When the trial resumed, Alice concluded her testimony with a strong denial of Rorech's account of her confession.

The decision to permit Alice to testify gave prosecutor Lombardino the opportunity he had been waiting for: to question her closely about her love life. All the most titillating incidents were brought out: the night Eddie had caught her in bed with the amorous waiter Carl Andrade, an afternoon tryst with a buyer at the World's Fair, a 1964 cruise with Tony Grace to the Democratic National Convention in Atlantic City, and nude swimming at Joe Rorech's home when, Lombardino was careful to stress, the children were dead. To reporter Kenneth Gross it seemed that Lombardino had torn away the last shred of Alice's dignity when he enquired whether she remembered making love with her children's barber in the back of a car behind the barbershop; Alice admitted having had ten dates with the barber, but, straining at a gnat, couldn't recall the incident in the car. Lombardino continued the catalogue of Alice's conquests with obvious relish until the judge ordered him to conclude.

The trial ended after thirteen days on Monday 27 May, and early the next morning the jury returned a verdict of guilty of manslaughter in the first degree; one of the jurors said that a large majority had voted for conviction on the first ballot, but that he had doubts about the proof and did not regard her as a danger to society. At her sentencing hearing, Alice protested her innocence and angrily told Judge Farrell, 'You don't care who killed my children, you want to close your books. You don't give a damn who killed my kids.' The judge sentenced her to be confined in the New York State prison for women at Westfield State Farms, Bedford Hills, New York, for a term of not less than five nor more than twenty years.

Alice's conviction was far from the last chapter of the case. In December 1969 the Appellate Division of the New York Supreme Court, an intermediate appeals court, ordered a new trial because three of the jurors had secretly visited the scene of Sophie Earomirski's identification of Alice. One of the jurors had made his visit alone at about two in the morning, hoping to verify what Sophie could have seen at that hour. The court reasoned that 'the net effect of the jurors' visits was that they made themselves secret, untested witnesses not subject to any cross-examination'. The State's highest court, the Court of Appeals, agreed, ruling in April 1970 that the unauthorised visits were inherently prejudicial to the defendant, and adding, in a significant aside, that the evidence of guilt 'was not so overwhelming that we can say, as a matter of law, that the error could not have influenced the verdict'. The Court noted that only two witnesses, Sophie Earomirski and Joe Rorech, had directly implicated Alice, and that Rorech's testimony 'was seriously challenged, and the witness was subjected to searching cross-examination'.

When the case was retried in 1971, a change in counsel and the presiding judge and the cooling of community passions resulted in a more restrained courtroom atmosphere. Gone from the prosecution team was Tony Lombardino, replaced by Thomas Demakos, the experienced chief of the District Attorney's trial bureau. The judge to whom the second trial was assigned, George Balbach, planted court attendants in the courtroom and adjacent corridors to assure better order. Perhaps the most significant change was at the defence table, where Herbert Lyon, a leader of the Queens trial bar, now sat in the first chair. Lyon had devised a more conservative defence plan, intended to place greater stress on Alice's grief and loss, and to keep her off the witness stand so that the prejudicial parade of her love affairs could not be repeated.

The stakes had been raised in the second trial, which began on Monday, 15 March 1971. As Alice's first jury had found her guilty of manslaughter in the death of Missy, principles of double jeopardy prohibited her from being charged with a greater offence against her daughter, but the prosecution had compensated for that limitation by obtaining an additional indictment for the murder of young Eddie. Though the state of his remains ruled out proof of cause of death, Demakos offered the evidence of Dr Milton Helpern that murder could be 'inferred' because of the circumstances of his sister's death. Joe Rorech, obliging as ever, adapted his testimony to the new prosecution design; according to his revised story, Alice had told him that she had killed Missy and 'consented' to the murder of her son.

The presentation of defence evidence was already in progress when Demakos, over vigorous objection by Lyon, was permitted to bring a surprise witness to the stand. Mrs Tina DeVita, a resident of the Kew Gardens Hills development at the time of the crime, testified that on the night of 13/14 July, while driving home with her husband, she had looked out of the driver's window from the passenger's side and seen 'people walking, a man carrying a bundle, a woman, a dog, and a boy'. The angry Lyon could not shake Mrs DeVita's story but did much to neutralise its impact by introducing an unheralded witness of his own, Marvin Weinstein, a young salesman from Massapequa, Long Island. Weinstein swore that on the morning of 14 July he, together with his wife, son and daughter, had passed below Sophie Earomirski's window on the way to his car; he had carried his daughter under his arm 'like a sack' and they were accompanied by their dog – who might well have looked pregnant for she had long ago lost her figure. As a final jab at the State's case, Lyon called Vincent Colabella, a jailed gangster who had reportedly admitted to a fellow prisoner that he had been Eddie's executioner, only to deny that report when questioned by the police. On the stand Colabella chuckled as he disowned any knowledge of the crime; he said that he had never seen Alice Crimmins before.

In his closing argument, Lyon cited Sophie Earomirski's testimony that she had been led to tell her story by the voices of the children crying from the grave; if they were crying, Alice's defence lawyer suggested, they were saying, 'Let my mother go; you have had her long enough!' Demakos had harsher words, reminding the jury of Alice's failure to take the stand, 'She doesn't have the courage to stand up here and tell the world she killed her daughter.' Alice interrupted to protest, 'Because I didn't!' but the prosecutor went on without being put off his stroke, 'And the shame and pity of it is that this little boy had to die too.'

The jury deliberations began after lunch on Thursday 23 April and ended at 5.45 p.m. on the following day. Alice was found guilty of murder in the first degree in the death of her son and of manslaughter in the strangling of Missy.

On 13 May 1971 Alice Crimmins was remanded to Bedford Hills prison, and there she stayed for two years while her lawyers continued the battle for her freedom in the appellate courts. In May 1973 the Appellate Division ruled for a second time in her favour. The court threw out the murder conviction on the grounds that the State had not proved beyond reasonable doubt that young Eddie's death had resulted from a criminal act. With respect to the manslaughter count relating to Missy, the court ordered a new trial on the basis of a number of errors and improprieties, including the prosecutor's comment that Alice lacked the courage to admit the killing of Missy: this argument amounted to an improper assertion that the prosecutor knew her to be guilty and, in addition, was an improper attack on her refusal to testify. Alice was freed from prison following this ruling, but the rejoicing in her camp was premature. The tortuous path of the judicial proceedings had two more dangerous corners.

The first setback was suffered when the Court of Appeals in February 1975 announced its final decision in the appeals relating to the verdicts in the second trial. The court sustained the decision of the Appellate Division only in part: it agreed with the dismissal of the murder charge but reversed the grant of a new trial in the manslaughter conviction for the killing of Missy, returning that issue to the Appellate Division for reconsideration. Explaining the latter ruling, the Court of Appeals conceded that Demakos's comment on Alice's refusal to testify violated her constitutional privilege against self-incrimination. However, in seeming contradiction of its sceptical view of the prosecution case in the first trial, the court decided that the constitutional error was harmless in view of the weighty evidence of Alice's guilt.

The Appellate Division confirmed the manslaughter conviction in May 1975, and Alice was once again sent back to prison to continue serving her sentence of from five to twenty years. Persevering in his efforts for her vindication, Lyon still had one card to play, an appeal from the denial of his motion for retrial, based on newly discovered evidence. A would-be witness, an electronics scientist named F. Sutherland Macklem, had given the defence an affidavit to the effect that, shortly after one o'clock on the morning of 14 July 1965, he had picked up two small children, a boy and a girl, hitchhiking in Queens County. The boy had told him he knew where his home was, and Macklem had let them out, safe and sound, at the corner of 162nd Street and 71st Avenue. The affiant did not learn the children's names, but stated that the boy could well have identified his companion as 'Missy' instead of 'my sister', as he had first thought. He admitted that he had identified his passengers as the Crimmins children only after reading newspaper accounts of the first trial, three years after the incident.

On 22 December 1975, the New York Court of Appeals affirmed the trial court's rejection of this defence initiative. The court was influenced by the affiant's seven year delay in coming forward, and commented scathingly that the affidavit 'offers an imaginative alternative hypothetical explanation [of the crime], worthy of concoction by an A. Conan Doyle'.

In January 1976 Alice Crimmins became eligible for a work-release programme and was permitted to leave prison on week days to work as a secretary. In August 1977 the New York *Post* reported that Alice had spent the previous Sunday 'as she has spent many balmy summer Sundays of her prison-term – on a luxury cruiser at City Island'. (Under the work-release programme, participants were allowed every other weekend at liberty.) In July 1977, Alice married the proprietor of the luxury cruiser, her contractor boyfriend, Anthony Grace. The *Post* was indignant over the nuptials, furnishing telephoto shots of Alice in a bikini and T-shirt, and headlining a follow-up story with a comment of the Queens District Attorney, 'Alice should be behind bars!'

On 7 September 1977, Alice Crimmins was granted parole, after thirty months in prison and nine months in the work-release programme. When a new petition for retrial was denied in November, she slipped into what must have been welcome obscurity; she had become that stalest of all commodities, old news.

The Crimmins case remains an intractable puzzle. In his opening argument in the second trial, Herbert Lyon invited the jury to regard the case as a troubling mystery that had not been solved. It is always difficult to persuade the community to live at ease with an unknown murderer, but never more so than when a child or spouse has been killed and the evidence suggests that the household was the scene of the crime or of the victim's disappearance. As in the Lindbergh kidnapping or the murder of Julia Wallace, there is a strong tendency to suspect an 'inside job'. Alice Crimmins, who slept close by but claimed to have heard nothing out of the ordinary during the murder night, naturally came under suspicion. She was a mother (perhaps harbouring the nameless daily hostilities familiar to the annals of family murder) and the only adult living in the Kew Gardens Hills apartment, and she had the opportunity to commit the crime – but can anything more be said to justify the certainty the investigators showed from the start that she was guilty? If we reject the equation that the State of New York made between sexuality and murderousness, it appears that Alice displayed only one suspicious trait: despite her avowed grief over her lost children, she does not seem to have shown much interest in helping the authorities to identify the killer. Even this curious passivity may have been due to the defensive posture into which she was immediately thrust by police antagonism and surveillance, and she may also have genuinely believed that the murderer was not to be found in her circle of acquaintances, however wide and casual.

The prosecution never attributed a plausible motive to Alice. The presence of Missy and young Eddie in the apartment does not seem to have inhibited Alice's amorous adventures, but if she found the children to be under foot, she could easily have surrendered custody to her husband. It was rumoured that she had never liked Missy much, that she had killed her in anger and then called for underworld help to dispose of her son as an inconvenient witness. Under those circumstances it is hard to visualise the boy going willingly to his doom, a docile figure in the peaceful domestic procession belatedly recalled by Sophie Earomirski in which the murderers and their future victim were accompanied by a pregnant dog. If the theory of sudden anger did not sell, the police investigators were likely to fall back on Alice's own words, that she would rather see her children dead than lose them to Eddie in the pending custody battle. Alice enjoyed a tactical advantage as a mother in possession of the children, and there is no reason to conclude that, despite the lessened optimism she detected in her lawyer's voice during their conversation before the children's disappearance, the prospect was hopeless or that she thought so. If the uncertainty of the divorce court's ruling provided a viable motive, the police had as good a reason to charge Eddie with the crime, but they never took him seriously as a suspect.

In the mind of Joe Rorech, the theory of underworld involvement in the murder of Alice's son took on an even more sinister tone. After the second trial he told New York *Post* reporter George Carpozi Jr that Alice 'had to have those children out of the way to avoid the custody proceedings' that were to have been held on 21 July 1965. He spelled out his belief that Alice had arranged for three of her girlfriends to sleep with a prominent New York politician, who was afraid that the details of his indiscretion would come out at the custody hearing. Therefore, the man, who was 'deeply involved in New York politics and relied almost solely on the Democratic organisation for his bread and butter', had called on his gangland connections to eliminate the children, thereby averting the hearing. Rorech had no satisfactory answer when Carpozi asked him why the same objective could not have been accomplished with less pain to Alice by the murder of her estranged husband. Rorech's theory also fails to explain why the politician's scandal was deemed more likely to be publicised in a custody hearing than in the course of a murder investigation that was bound to focus on Alice Crimmins and her florid love life.

If Alice was in fact guilty, the reason for her crime must, despite the best surmises of the police and Joe Rorech, remain wrapped in mystery. Even more puzzling, though, is the autopsy evidence regarding Missy's last meal, which raises doubts concerning the time and place of the child's murder. This strange facet of the case was prominently featured in the dissenting opinion rendered by Justice Fuchsberg when the New York State Court of Appeals rejected Alice's motion for a new trial in 1975. Justice Fuchsberg noted that the testimony of the Queens medical examiner, Dr Richard Grimes, indicated that Missy had died shortly after ingesting a meal including a macaroni-like substance that differed substantially from the last dinner that Alice had told the police she served the children. This evidence suggested to the judge that 'the child might have had another meal at some unknown time and unknown place considerably after the one taken at home'.

Could Alice Crimmins have been so cunning a criminal planner as to have created this enigma by lying to the police about the food she had served on the night of the crime? Apart from the difficulty of finding traits of calculation and foresight in her character, many circumstances militate against the inference that the veal dinner was a fabrication intended by Alice to mislead the investigation. When she first mentioned the purchase of the frozen veal to Detective Piering, neither of the children's bodies had been found. If she was the murderer and had hidden the corpses, she had reason to hope that they would long remain undiscovered. Even if she feared the worst – that the victims would soon be found – it seems doubtful that she was so familiar with the capabilities of forensic medicine that she decided to turn to her own account the possibility that an autopsy might be performed in time to analyse the contents of the last meal.

There would have been a powerful deterrent to Alice's lying about the veal dinner. She told Piering that she had purchased the veal on the afternoon of 13 July in a neighbourhood delicatessen; she was presumably well known there, and the grocer who had waited on her could very likely have contradicted her story. As events turned out, the grocer did not remember what she had purchased, but she could not have counted on that in advance.

If the Crimmins case is viewed with the hindsight of the 1980s – when a young mother with a strong sexual appetite is less likely to be pronounced a Medea – it seems that Alice is entitled to the benefit of the Scottish verdict: Not Proven.

# A Slight Case of Arsenical Poisoning
### Jonathan Goodman

If the little old lady with a face as wrinkled as a walnut
had not been so fond of cats, her corpse might have lain
for days, even weeks, without being found. The only
person who called regularly at the squalid shack in the
woodlands near the village of South Kent, Connecticut,
was a local farmer, delivering milk for the dozen or more
cats that the woman known as Mrs Florence Chandler
had caught straying or merely strolling and brought home
with her. On an autumn morning in 1941, the farmer,
getting no reply to his knocking, pushed open the door
and, holding his breath against the stench, entered the
shack. 'The woman of the woods' lay crumpled on the
bed. Her eyes were wide open, staring at the ceiling, and
*rigor mortis* had stretched her lips into what looked like
a smile.

For the last half-century of her life, she had had
precious little to smile about. Things might have been
very different if only –

But no: I must tell her story from its beginning, leaving
you to decide whether she was a cold-blooded murderess,
fully deserving her dreadful fate, or an innocent victim of
cruel chance.

Florence Elizabeth Chandler was born in the September of 1862, the second year of the American Civil War,
in Mobile, Alabama, the bustling yet still gracious port
from which much of the raw cotton for the mills of
Lancashire and Cheshire was shipped.

She was only a few months old when her father, a

lawyer employed by a firm of commission merchants in the cotton trade, suddenly contracted a puzzling illness and died. For some time, there had been tittle-tattle about his wife Caroline's dalliance with some of his male friends – one in particular, a dashing Confederate Officer named Franklin Du Barry. Now the gossip became a sort of corroboration of the rumour that Caroline had used poison so as to achieve widowhood. The rumour was so strong, the nature of Mr Chandler's fatal illness so mysterious, that the police considered starting an investigation. Nothing came of this, however, and shortly after the funeral Caroline took herself and her children – baby Florence and her slightly older brother Holbrook – to the town in the adjoining state of Georgia where Captain Du Barry happened to be stationed. Caroline and the captain wasted no time in getting wed.

Marriage doesn't seem to have agreed with Franklin Du Barry. As a bachelor, he had rarely suffered a day's illness; within months of marrying Caroline, he developed a puzzling illness of a debilitating nature, and went downhill fast. One doctor who attended him hazarded a guess that he was suffering from consumption; others pooh-poohed that notion, pointing to symptoms that were at variance with it. Various nostrums were prescribed, but none did the slightest good. At last, in the spring of 1864, he was granted six months' leave of absence to go to Europe 'for the benefit of his health'. The change of scene was Caroline's idea; hers alone. Du Barry, weak and emaciated by now, had no say in the matter. Caroline refused to listen to his doctors, who warned her that he would not survive the voyage.

The couple, with the two children, set sail for Scotland on a paddle-steamer called the *Fanny*. There was no doctor on board. Caroline again became a widow when the vessel was two days out of port. According to subsequent newspaper reports, the master of the *Fanny* wanted to turn back so that Du Barry's body could be submitted to a coroner's jury, but Caroline insisted on burial at sea.

As both her dead husbands had willed her all their

worldly goods, she was pretty well off. After completing the voyage to Greenock, she lived in England for a short time, then moved to Paris, where she and the children resided for several years. In the early 1870s, following a number of love affairs, some of which were concurrent, she married a Prussian cavalry officer, Baron Adolph von Roques.

She paid a high price for the title of Baroness. When von Roques was drunk, which was frequently, he beat her; he forced her to assist him in confidence tricks and frauds, and, having got his hands on most of what was left of her legacies, abandoned her.

But Caroline was nothing if not resilient. And she had learnt a lot from the roguish von Roques – for instance, how to use a title as collateral for loans that she had no intention of repaying. With Florence in tow (Holbrook was now studying medicine in Paris), the Baroness led a butterfly existence, flitting between Europe and the re-United States – and, supposing a newspaper story to be true, at one time turning up in the Middle East, where for a few weeks or months she 'filled the equivocal position of the wife of an attaché of the British Legation in Tehran.'

In March 1880, she and Florence, who was now seventeen, travelled from New York to Liverpool on a White Star liner, the *Baltic*. On the first evening of the voyage, they were escorted to the bar by an elderly man from New Orleans who had been a friend of Caroline's first husband. Having sized up the other male passengers in the bar, she set her cap at a man of about her own age.

He wasn't handsome, but he looked prosperous. Reasonably tall, he had a florid complexion, slightly staring grey eyes, and a blond head of hair, much lighter than the moustache that drooped around his small mouth. His name, the Baroness quickly discovered, was James Maybrick. A few discreet enquiries confirmed her impression of his prosperity: he was a leading English cotton broker, with fine offices in Tithebarn Street, in the centre of Liverpool. At forty, he was still a bachelor.

Maybrick accepted the Baroness's invitation to join her at her table. He talked animatedly. But not to the Baroness. His attention was directed at her daughter Florence. Clearly, he was captivated.

One can understand why. On the threshold of woman-hood, Florence was a surprising but appealing mixture of shyness and sophistication; life with mother had given her a precocious worldly-wisdom but at the same time had made her unconfident of herself and of people who showed interest in her. She had golden hair, naturally curly, her eyes were a striking violet-blue, and, though she was quite short, she had a voluptuous body.

As the dinner-gong sounded, Maybrick, the perfect gentleman, asked the Baroness if she had any objection to his requesting the pleasure of her daughter's company when he strolled on the deck the next morning. Hiding her huffishness at the fact that Maybrick had not suc-cumbed to her own charms, the Baroness glanced at Florence, saw that she was nodding eagerly, imploringly, and gave her assent.

The stroll was the first of many. By the middle of the voyage, the couple were constant companions, and on the night before the *Baltic* docked at Liverpool, Maybrick expressed his love for Florence, and she spoke of her deep fondness for him. With the Baroness's approval, it was agreed that, if they still felt the same way after six months, during which Maybrick would pursue his business ventures in the North of England and Florence would be with her mother on the Continent, they should plan marriage.

In the autumn of 1880, Florence accepted a diamond engagement ring from James Maybrick, and on 27 July of the following year they were united in holy matrimony at a fashionable London church.

Before the marriage and during the honeymoon at Bournemouth, James Maybrick told Florence quite a lot about himself. Quite a lot, but by no means everything.

Talking of people for whom he felt affection, he mentioned his four brothers, making particular reference

87

to Michael, who was a successful musical performer and composer (under the pseudonym of 'Stephen Adams', he wrote the tunes of several popular hymns, including *The Holy City* and *Star of Bethlehem*), and Edwin, the youngest, who was James's junior partner in the cotton-broking firm of Maybrick & Co. But he did not mention that he had had a mistress in Liverpool for nearly twenty years, a woman who had borne him five children, all of whom had died in infancy or childhood.

He admitted that he was fearful of illness. But he did not intimate that his hypochondria caused him to dose himself with so many quack remedies that an American business acquaintance had once exclaimed, 'Maybrick has got a dozen drug stores in his stomach.' Nor did he admit that, since 1877, when he was treated for a real illness with arsenic and strychnine, he had used individually small amounts of those toxic substances as preventive medicines.

He said that he derived great pleasure from attendance at race meetings. But he did not tell Florence that, lately, he had had to restrict his punting because Maybrick & Co. was going through a bad patch.

Florence soon learned that James had financial worries. He refused to make a marriage settlement, and though he agreed to set up a trust fund for her and any offspring, never got round to doing it. He did, however, take out life insurance, first for £2,000 and later for an additional £2,500, with her as beneficiary.

If she hoped that, after the nomadic existence with her mother, she could now settle down, she was disappointed. For the first three years, at any rate. During that time, the Maybricks travelled back and forth between Liverpool and the cotton states of America, never having a permanent home despite the fact that, in March 1882, slightly less than eight months after the wedding, Florence gave birth to a son, James Chandler, nicknamed 'Bobo'. (Four years later, a daughter, Gladys Evelyn, was born.)

They returned to Liverpool for good in 1884. James rented a house near Sefton Park from an old friend of his family, a formidable woman named Matilda Briggs, two of whose sisters had entertained hopes of marrying James and were therefore only too eager to note faults in Florence as a wife and mother. In 1888, the Maybricks moved to another rented house but a much larger one. This was Battlecrease House, in the suburb of Aigburth, about five miles from the centre of Liverpool. The house, which was of three storeys, containing some twenty rooms, would soon become the setting of a tragedy – perhaps the scene of a murder.

Although, in those days, domestic servants received pathetically small recompense for excessively long hours of work, Maybrick's employment of five – a cook, a couple of maids, a gardener, and a nanny for the children – suggests that his financial position had improved. Even so, he frequently berated Florence for overspending on the household budget he had set, and for what he considered extravagance in the clothes she bought for herself and the children. In one of several unhappy letters to her mother, she wrote:

I am utterly worn out and in such a state of overstrained nervousness I am hardly fit for anything. Whenever the doorbell rings I feel ready to faint for fear it is someone coming to have an account paid, and when Jim comes home at night it is with fear and trembling that I look into his face to see whether anyone has been to the office about my bills . . . my life is a continual state of fear of something or somebody.

Money was not the only thing they quarrelled over. When Florence learned that Maybrick was dosing himself with drugs and quack potions, she warned him of possible dire consequences, but was told to shut up. After further arguments, she informed Maybrick's doctor that he was taking 'some very strong medicine which has a bad influence on him', then wrote to Michael Maybrick that his brother was taking a 'white powder' that she suspected was the cause of the headaches he was always complaining about. She also spoke to her own doctor about the white powder, saying that she thought it was strychnine. The doctor told her, 'Well, if your husband should ever die suddenly, call me and I can say that you have had some conversation with me about it.'

The most bitter arguments arose when Florence discovered that not only had James kept a mistress before his marriage but that he was still consorting with the woman in Liverpool, Manchester and Chester.

Perhaps thinking along sauce-for-the-gander lines (or was it an inheritance of her mother's promiscuity?), Florence had affairs with other men, including her brother-in-law Edwin. Only one of the affairs, the last of them, seems to have been at all serious. It certainly had serious repercussions.

Alfred Brierley was a handsome, bearded cotton-broker, fifteen years younger than his friend James Maybrick and eight years older than Florence, who in November 1888, when she had her first secret assignation with Brierley, was twenty-six. It appears that after he had made the advances and had led Florence to expect more than a run-of-the-bedroom sex-capade, he turned out to be what is known nowadays as a prize tease. When the affair was over, curtailed by happenings at Battlecrease House that required Florence's full attention, she said of Brierley, 'He piqued my vanity and resisted my efforts to please him.'

In March 1889, Florence did a very silly thing – or rather, did something in a very silly way. She reserved a suite at a London hotel, Flatman's, which was a favourite of cotton men from the North – and, compounding the idiocy of her choice of hotel, told the booking clerk that the accommodation was for 'Mr and Mrs Thomas Maybrick of Manchester'. She arrived at Flatman's (which was in Henrietta Street, close to Covent Garden) on a Thursday, and Brierley came later in the day and stayed with her till lunchtime on the Sunday.

Soon after her return to Liverpool, she accompanied Maybrick to the Grand National. Brierley was there, too. And so was the Prince of Wales – present because the

90

steeplechase was being run for the fiftieth time. When the race was over, Brierley approached Florence and, taking her by the arm, escorted her to the grandstand to see the royal party. Maybrick was furious.

That evening, back at Battlecrease House, the Maybricks had a violent quarrel, each accusing the other of infidelity. Florence ran into the hall and shouted at a servant to call her a cab. But her husband dragged her into the drawing-room, where he tore her clothes and beat her, leaving her with a black eye.

A fortnight later, Maybrick went to London. While dining with his brother Michael, he mentioned that he was not feeling well, and Michael arranged for his own doctor to examine him. Maybrick told the doctor that he was suffering from pains in the head and numbness of the limbs; he said that he was apprehensive of paralysis. Finding nothing seriously wrong with him, the doctor gave him prescriptions for three 'tonics', mere placebos, to be made up in Liverpool.

Within three weeks of his return to Battlecrease House, James Maybrick was dead.

Mud-packs, egg whites, scented creams, concoctions of honey, draught Guinness and lemon juice – those are just a few of the things that women have been known to spread on their faces in the hope of enhancing their complexions. I don't suppose that, these days, many women knowingly moisten their features with dilutions of arsenic; but in the 1880s that poison was reckoned to be a sure means of bringing a bloom to wan cheeks. It is surprising how often, when reading accounts of murders and scandals of the period, one comes across references to ardent but dyspeptic beaux, and one cannot help wondering whether the indigestion was a side-effect of tongue-out-of-cheek passion.

Florence Maybrick certainly used arsenic as a cosmetic when she was in her late teens, still single. Perhaps she intended to try it again in April 1889, three months before the eighth anniversary of her wedding to James Maybrick.

91

On the 23rd of that month, a Tuesday, she bought a dozen arsenic-tainted flypapers from a chemist with whom she had an account. Rather than asking for the purchase to be slated, she paid cash; and rather than simply popping the flypapers in her bag, requested the chemist (who was no more obliging than other shopkeepers at that time) to get his errand-boy to deliver them to Battlecrease House. She told the chemist that 'flies were beginning to be troublesome in the kitchen' – a remark that surprised him, considering the coolness of the spring – but, in fact, as soon as the flypapers were delivered, she took them to her bedroom, unrolled them, and put them in a basin of water to soak. It must be said that she did that without apparent stealth, leaving the basin, covered by a plate, in full view of servants who entered the room.

On 25 April, James Maybrick drew up a new will. It appears that either his chronic hypochondria had become acute or he had a premonition of imminent death, for at the start of the rather incoherent document, he noted that he was writing it 'in case I die before having made a regular and proper will in legal form'. So as not to seem uncharitable, he mentioned that his wife would benefit from insurance policies – and then cut her off without a penny, leaving all his possessions in trust for their two children. He hoped that Florence would stay with the children at Battlecrease House 'so long as she remains a widow'.

Two days later, on the Saturday, he had an attack of vomiting, and complained that his limbs felt numb. However, he must have felt better by the afternoon, because he insisted on going to the Wirral Races. Not surprisingly, since he wandered about the course during a rainstorm, he developed a chill; in the evening, dining with friends, his hands were so atremble that he spilled his wine.

The following day, he felt worse. Or so he said. The trouble with Maybrick was that he had cried wolf so often, over so many years, that people might have worried that something was badly wrong with him if, just for once, he had said that he felt as fit as fiddle. Anyway, the doctor was called. Before seeing Maybrick, he spoke with Florence, who, as she had done in the past, expressed concern about a white powder that she said her husband was taking. The doctor diagnosed a stomach upset, and put Maybrick on a bland diet. The diagnosis did not satisfy Maybrick. During the afternoon, he scribbled a letter to his brother Michael, saying that if he died from whatever it was that was wrong with him, a post-mortem examination should be carried out.

But next day – Monday, 29 April – even he had to admit that he felt a lot better. Florence left the house to do some shopping. Visiting a different chemist from the one she had patronised six days before, she bought a couple of dozen flypapers and a bottle of face lotion. It was a quite complicated transaction: she paid for the flypapers and took them with her, but put the cost of the lotion on her account and asked for the bottle to be delivered.

Maybrick went back to work on the Tuesday. On the following two days, he stayed in his office at lunchtime, devouring jugs of a patent food, consisting mainly of lentil-meal, that had been made up by his wife. The stuff was called Du Barry's Revalenta Arabica; whoever the brand-naming Du Barry was, he was unrelated to the military one who had been Florence's first step-father.

Maybrick became ill again on Friday, 3 May. Now he was suffering from 'deep-seated pains' in the legs. The doctor, summoned to Battlecrease House, gave him morphine. That relieved the pains, but on both the Saturday and the Sunday he had a number of severe attacks of vomiting. Next day, the doctor visited him again, and this time prescribed Fowler's solution, a common remedy that was a mixture of 1 per cent white arsenic with carbonate of potash. At Florence's suggestion, a nurse was engaged and the doctor arranged for a colleague to come along to give a second opinion.

Her husband's condition was not the only thing Florence had on her mind: she had just received a letter from

Alfred Brierley, dead scared that Maybrick might find out about their suite-sharing at Flatman's, and insisting that they should not meet till – all being well – the autumn.

In the afternoon of Wednesday, 8 May, Florence did two things, one following on from the other, that she would regret for the rest of her life. While sitting at her husband's bedside, she wrote a reply to Brierley, then gave the letter to Alice Yapp, the children's nanny, to post.

Yapp was aptly named. Since entering the Maybricks' service, she had continually gossiped about her mistress – and recently, after being jilted, she had become resentful and malicious towards her. Shortly before being given the letter to post, she had been out of the house, enjoying a tongue-wagging session with Matilda Briggs, who still bore a grudge against Florence for having blighted her hope that one of her sisters would become Mrs James Maybrick. Following the session, during which Yapp had voiced a dreadful inference from Florence's purchases of flypapers, Mrs Briggs had sent a telegram to Michael Maybrick in London:

'COME AT ONCE. STRANGE THINGS GOING ON HERE.'

On the way to the Aigburth post office, Yapp contrived to drop Florence's letter to Brierley in a puddle, thus giving her an excuse to take the letter from the envelope. Her gaze just happened to alight on certain words and phrases: 'Dearest . . .', 'my own darling . . .', '[James] is sick unto death.' Without further ado, she handed the letter to Edwin Maybrick. And he – unaware of the action taken by Matilda Briggs – telegraphed his brother Michael to come at once.

Michael Maybrick arrived at Battlecrease House that evening. Straightway after reading the letter to Brierley, he took charge of things, telling the nurse that she alone should administer to James, ordering the servants to watch Florence's every move, and keeping an eye on her himself. On Friday, 10 May, he thought he saw her transferring a liquid of some sort from one bottle to another, and shouted at her, 'Florie, how dare you tamper with the medicine!'

By then, it was clear that James Maybrick was dying; doctors continued to wander in and out of the sickroom, but they gave only a pretence of treatment. The end came at half past eight on the Saturday evening, shortly after Maybrick's children – but not his wife – had been taken to kiss him goodbye.

Later that night and on the following morning, while Florence lay in a drug-induced sleep, Michael and Edwin, energetically assisted by Alice Yapp and Matilda Briggs, searched the house from top to bottom. Yapp scored the first success: rummaging in one of her mistress's trunks, she found a packet of powder labelled 'ARSENIC: POISON FOR CATS'. After more arsenic had been found in divers places, Michael Maybrick took Matilda Briggs's advice and invited a police superintendent to call at Battlecrease House.

The doctors who had attended James Maybrick believed that he had died from gastro-enteritis. But, what with all the gossip contrary to that belief, they decided that a post-mortem examination should be performed before a death certificate was issued. The examination, performed on Monday, 13 May, revealed (*a*) inflammation of certain organs, (*b*) traces of arsenic – traces so slight that they could not be weighed.

Next day, despite those equivocal findings, Police Superintendent Isaac Bryning, the senior investigator at the house, went into the room where Florence Maybrick was lying and told her that she was in custody on suspicion of having caused her husband's death. Soon afterwards, Matilda Briggs, who was pottering about the house as if she owned it, sat herself down by the widow's bedside and happily chatted away about what she had picked up by eavesdropping on conversations between the official investigators. The most important news imparted by Matilda was that traces of arsenic had been found in the jug that had contained Maybrick's lunch of proprietary slop on the last day he had spent at his office. She asked if it was true that Florence had prepared the meal. Before Florence had a chance to reply, a spoilsport policeman insisted that there should be no further conversation on matters relating to the case.

Later, when Florence mentioned that she had no money for stamps or telegrams, and so was unable to communicate with friends other than Matilda, the latter could not resist suggesting that she should get in touch with Alfred Brierley and ask him for financial assistance. Seemingly unaware that Matilda was being sarcastic, Florence scribbled a begging letter to her erstwhile lover, handed it to Matilda to post – and was surprised when her 'friend' scampered out of the room to give the incriminating letter to Superintendent Bryning.

It was not until near the end of the week that Florence was able to persuade Michael Maybrick to send telegrams to her mother, the Baroness von Roques, in Paris.

With a relative like her mother, Florence hardly needed enemies. As soon as the Baroness arrived at Battlecrease House, she behaved like someone looking for a quarrel. An argument with one of the Maybrick brothers was so fierce and loud that Florence, awoken by it, became hysterical, and a quartet of policemen rushed into her room to help a nurse hold her down on the bed. The Baroness rushed after them, shouting that it was disgraceful for men to enter a lady's boudoir without permission. As the shame-faced constables retreated she turned on the nurse, screaming, 'I know more of nursing than you do. If you'll let me hold her hand and speak to her, she will be calm.' But she had met her match in the burly nurse-cum-guard, who threatened to carry her from the room if she didn't leave of her own accord. The Baroness's exit-line – 'Better death than such dishonour!' – was uttered so thunderously that it was heard by everyone in the house, including Isaac Bryning, who was down in the kitchen. Misinterpreting the declamation as meaning that the Baroness intended to administer poison to her daughter so as to keep her out of a common cell, the superintendent gave orders for Florence to be taken to Walton Gaol, on the outskirts of Liverpool.

After the body of James Maybrick had been exhumed and further traces of arsenic found in it, a coroner's jury returned a verdict of murder against Florence Maybrick.

The case was front-page news in English papers before the Baroness appeared on the scene. With her arrival, reporters for American papers took an interest. In Alabama, someone working on the Mobile *Daily Register* recalled that, a quarter of a century before, the woman who was now the Baroness von Roques had been suspected of murdering her first two husbands. The *Register's* rehash of what had happened – or of what some residents of Mobile *thought* had happened – was reprinted in English papers. The implication was clear: *Poisoning ran in the family*.

That story – and others (for instance, that Mrs Maybrick, pregnant by Brierley, had suffered a miscarriage in prison: quite untrue) – must have been taken into consideration by her legal advisers when they discussed whether or not to request that she be tried in London rather than Liverpool. Though the prejudice against her was particularly strong in Liverpool, they decided not to ask for a change of venue, and the trial opened at St George's Hall on the last day of July.

Despite having had to scratch around for funds to pay for the defence, Mrs Maybrick's solicitor had acquired the services of two of the most brilliant barristers in England: Sir Charles Russell and William Pickford (who would become, respectively, Lord Chief Justice and Master of the Rolls). In comparison, the prosecution team, led by a local Queen's Counsel named John Addison, seemed second-rate. Before the trial, people who had decided that Mrs Maybrick was guilty complained of the disparity between the advocatory skills of the two sets of lawyers.

They needn't have worried. As it turned out, they had an influential ally in court. No less a person than the judge, Mr Justice Stephen. It was well known that

Stephen was unbendingly moral. What was known to only a few was that he was in the early stages of lunacy. Two years later, he would be locked up in an asylum.

The trial was, for those times, a long-drawn-out affair, lasting seven days. The prosecution case had two main weaknesses. Sufficient arsenic had been discovered scattered around Battlecrease House to poison almost the entire population of Aigburth – but only the arsenic smeared flypapers could be shown to have been purchased by Florence Maybrick. It had not even been possible to prove whether, let alone when, she had bought the packet of arsenic, labelled 'POISON FOR CATS' that had been found in one of her trunks. There was the further weakness that neither of the examinations of the body of James Maybrick had revealed more than slight traces of arsenic.

Mr Addison called a dozen or so witnesses to speak of events leading up to, and directly following, Maybrick's death: servants (among whom Alice Yapp was far and away the most loquacious), Maybrick's brothers, the doctors, and visitors to the house (it was clear from Matilda Brigg's evidence that she had for years acted in a two-faced way towards Florence, and had welcomed the chance of making trouble for her; a murmur of disapproval scurried round the court as she left the witness box).

The penultimate prosecution witness was Alfred Schweisso, the head waiter at Flatman's (whose testimony that he had seen the defendant and Brierley only once or twice while they were staying at the hotel was meant to show that they had taken only one or two breaks from what the defendant had booked a suite for them to do), and he was followed by the Crown's star witness, Dr Thomas Stevenson, the Home Office analyst. Stevenson asserted that, having analysed the internal organs removed during the post-mortem examinations of the body of James Maybrick, he had 'no doubts that this man died from the effects of arsenic'. When cross-examined by Sir Charles Russell, he admitted that he had found no sign that might not have been a sign of gastro-enteritis. Even so, he refused to budge from his opinion.

The defence called three medical men, one of them quite as prestigious as Stevenson, who contradicted just about everything Stevenson had said. All three believed that James Maybrick had died from gastro-enteritis. Russell also called a number of acquaintances of Maybrick, American as well as English, who testified that he had frequently taken potions containing arsenic, and a chemist from near the Liverpool Cotton Exchange who said that Maybrick had come into his shop 'several times a day' prior to the spring of 1888 to drink a prescribed pick-me-up containing 'liquor arsenicalis'.

When the last defence witness was gone, the judge allowed Mrs Maybrick to make a statement from the dock. Weeping as she spoke, her voice tremulous, she insisted that she had used the flypapers to make a face-wash; then, to the surprise of most people in court, she claimed that two nights before her husband's death, he had implored her to give him some white powder from a bottle on the table near the window, and she had consented.

After the closing speeches, first by Russell, then by Addison, Mr Justice Stephen summed up. He seemed perfectly sane at the start.

The summing-up lasted twelve hours, spread over two days, Tuesday and Wednesday, the 6th and 7th of July. On the Tuesday, Mr Justice Stephen made a number of factual errors – concerning, for instance the dates and times of incidents at Battlecrease House during the last fortnight or so of James Maybrick's life – but they were minor blemishes on a cogent and carefully phrased speech. Sir Charles Russell and the junior counsel for the defence must have been well pleased, for several of the judge's comments indicated that, in his view, the case for the prosecution was too frail to justify a verdict of Guilty.

At the end of the day, having reverted to the all-important question of how Maybrick had met his death

– whether from arsenical poisoning, the cause put forward by the Crown's medical expert, or from gastro-enteritis, according with the opinion of the doctors who had given evidence for the defence – Mr Justice Stephen virtually told the jury that the prosecution had failed to prove that a crime had been committed, 'We are there getting amongst questions which are really, speaking quite plainly, too difficult for us – at all events, they are too difficult for me.'

But it seems that, when Mr Justice Stephen returned to the judges' lodgings at Newsham House, his mind was in turmoil; the more he tried to concentrate on the legal aspects of the case, the more his thoughts swerved towards the sole unequivocal fact to emerge from the evidence: the fact that Mrs Maybrick had committed adultery – had broken the Eighth Commandment. According to the hearsay of Sir Henry Dickens, the novelist Charles's lawyer-son, 'That night Stephen's brother judge had a somewhat startling experience. Early in the morning he was awakened by Stephen, whom he found walking up and down in his room, saying as he did so, "That woman is guilty. That woman is guilty."'

Guilty of what?

Why, of *IMMORALITY*. The following day, Stephen's eyes stared, his voice shrieked, as he castigated the weeping woman in the dock for her relationship with Alfred Brierley – as he exclaimed that adultery, an awful crime in itself, was known to spawn other crimes. There was 'strong evidence', he told the jury, that Mrs Maybrick was 'actuated by a motive at once strong and disgraceful. . . . While her husband's life was trembling in the balance – even at that awful moment there arose in her heart and flowed from her pen various terms of endearment to the man with whom she had behaved so disgracefully. That was an awful thing to think of and a thing you will have to consider in asking yourselves whether she is guilty or not guilty.'

The jury needed only thirty-eight minutes to decide that, whatever crime Florence Maybrick had committed, she should be executed for it.

Predictably, as news of the verdict spread, first in this country then in America, politicians and editors of periodicals were deluged with letters, protest meetings and marches were organised, and people began collecting signatures to petitions for a reprieve; apart from Florence's mother, the Baroness von Roques, who undertook a gruelling round of press conferences, the busiest protesters were members of the fledging women's liberation movement, breaking off from the campaign for sexual equality to argue that, because of Mrs Maybrick's sex, it would be wrong to hang her.

The most influential protesters, because they were the most surprising ones, were the four 'unofficial investigators' who, between them, had come up with far more evidence against Mrs Maybrick than the police had subsequently been able to find. The dead man's brothers, Michael and Edwin, gave an interview to the press in which they said that 'nothing would please them more than to hear that the Home Secretary's decision is that Mrs Maybrick shall go free' (Michael may have been prompted to speak out on behalf of his sister-in-law by an article in the *Manchester Courier*, hinting that he might have been implicated in the poisoning of James Maybrick); Alice Yapp, the Maybrick children's nanny, who had created the suspicion about her mistress, chiefly by opening Florence's letter to Brierley and making its contents known, told a reporter, 'If I had only known that my action would place Mrs Maybrick where she is today, I would have torn the letter up, burned it, or done anything with it'; and even Matilda Briggs, Florence's most bitter enemy, claimed to be her most faithful friend.

The hullabaloo had an effect. As there was no court of appeal, Mrs Maybrick's only hope of escaping execution lay with the Home Secretary, Henry Matthews. The day after petitions with half a million signatures were dumped on Matthews' desk – and a week before the sentence was due to be carried out at Walton Jail – he conferred with Mr Justice Stephen, both sets of barristers, and the medical experts, and then announced his decision 'to respite the capital sentence on Florence Maybrick and to commute the punishment to penal servitude for life as, although the evidence leads clearly to the conclusion that the prisoner administered and attempted to administer arsenic to her husband with intent to murder, yet it does not wholly exclude a reasonable doubt whether his death was in fact caused by the administration of arsenic.'

There was great rejoicing. Not by Florence, though: when the prison governor told her the news, she simply nodded and shook his hand. Nor by members of the legal profession, who pointed out that the decision didn't make sense: Mrs Maybrick was to serve a life sentence for *attempted* murder – a charge on which she had not been tried and of which she had not been convicted.

Almost certainly, Matthews acted on the ground of political expediency; one of his Tory colleagues said at the time that the hanging of Mrs Maybrick would have cost the party a hundred thousand votes.

Queen Victoria, the Personification of moral rectitude, was not pleased with the decision. When she was told of it, prior to its being announced, she penned a note to Her secretary, Sir Henry Ponsonby: 'Would Sir Henry thank Mr Matthews and say the only regret she feels is that so wicked a woman should escape by a mere legal quibble! . . . The sentence must never be further commuted.'

The Queen got Her way. Despite the fact that, over the years, many leading public figures – including three successive Presidents of the United States – sought to have the sentence reduced, it was not until after the Queen's death, when Florence Maybrick had served over fourteen years, that a parole was granted.

After spending a short time in France, staying with her mother, Florence travelled to America, where she was greeted by crowds of well-wishers. She wrote her memoirs, saying much about her life in prison but little about the reason for her imprisonment, and then went on a lecture tour, which was interrupted when she entered into litigation concerning properties purchased by her maternal grandfather. She won the case but finished up out of pocket, because her opponent died without having paid her a penny. In 1911, soon after hearing of the death of her mother, she learned that her son – whom she had not seen since her arrest – had died in very strange circumstances. An engineer for a Canadian gold mine, he had lunched in his laboratory, sitting at a table on which there was a glass of water and a beaker of potassium cyanide; apparently he had drunk from the beaker by mistake.

During the next half dozen years, Florence led a vagrant existence. At one time she sold encyclopaedias door-to-door, at another she was looked after by the Salvation Army; occasionally, she received hand-outs from relatives or old friends.

In the mid-1930s, after working as a domestic servant, the woman who had once been the mistress of Battle-crease House, Liverpool, built herself a shack in the woods near the village of South Kent, Connecticut. Using her maiden name, Florence Chandler, she obtained a small state pension, just sufficient to support herself and her too many cats.

Florence was not a constant cat-lover. There was an occasion when, irritated by the cussedness of one of her feline lodgers, she poisoned the whole lot of them. I doubt if you will be surprised by the incidental information that the substance she administered was arsenic.

# The Carew Case
## Horace Wyndham

Wilkie Collins invented a 'Woman in White'. Edith Carew invented a 'Woman in Black'. Of the two, this latter was the greater mystery.

For people who want to discover one, a fairly close parallel exists between the case of Mrs Carew, which happened at Yokohama in 1896, and that of Mrs Maybrick, which happened at Liverpool in 1889. Each had points in common, and revolved round the 'eternal triangle'. Thus, a married couple of good social position, living 'double lives'; the husband dying suddenly; a coroner's inquest; and a widow convicted of administering arsenic. Also, anonymous letters and circumstantial evidence. In short, dramas of passion and poison, culminating in tragedy.

It was at a hunt ball, in the spring of 1889, that Edith Porch, the daughter of Mr James Porch, a prosperous merchant and the Mayor of Glastonbury, first met her future husband. This was Walter Raymond Hallowell Carew, son of Major Carew, of Exmouth. He was then thirty-six, and Edith Porch was fifteen years younger.

The wooing was a quick one, for the two were engaged after they had only met twice. Mr and Mrs Porch advanced a certain amount of opposition, for their daughter was something of an heiress, since she had £500 a year of her own, while Walter Carew had little beyond 'expectations'. However, as the couple were obviously very much in love with each other, they permitted the marriage to take place. Shortly afterwards, Carew

104

accepted a commercial appointment in Singapore; and, as it carried a good salary, his wife accompanied him there.

At first all went well; Edith Carew, charmed by the novelty of her surroundings, enjoyed herself to the full. Then, after two children had been born, she found the exile becoming wearisome. The subject of returning to England was often discussed, and it was practically settled that she should go home on a prolonged visit. Suddenly, however, Carew was offered an attractive position in Japan, and the family left for Yokohama (which was then a Treaty Port, open to foreign commerce).

Edith Carew did not regret the decision. She found the land of chrysanthemums and cherry-blossom much more attractive than the Straits Settlements. Also, the climate was much better. The European community in Yokohama, where they had a pleasant house on the Bluff, was a friendly one; and there was no lack of excursions, picnics, dances, and dinner-parties, etc., together with tennis and yachting. Mrs Carew, with her good looks and charm, was extremely popular; and Walter Carew, with his cheerful disposition, his social gifts, and his prowess at games, was asked to become secretary and manager of the United Club, where all the Europeans foregathered. This appointment, it is interesting to note in the light of what followed, was largely due to the personal recommendation of Mr John Lowder, a barrister practising in Yokohama.

Thus the years passed until the autumn of 1896. At that time, in addition to Mr and Mrs Carew and their family, a boy of five and a girl of six, the household consisted of Mrs Carew's brother, Reginald Porch, who had come out to the Far East on a visit, and Mary Esther Jacob, the children's nursery-governess. This young woman belonged to the same part of England as Mrs Carew, and had known her before her marriage.

To outward observers, the Carews appeared a thoroughly devoted couple. Still, little rifts manifested themselves occasionally. The cause was largely a financial one. Walter Carew had hospitable instincts. He liked to entertain lavishly, and to keep open house. As this meant spending much more than he earned, a considerable part of his wife's private income was absorbed.

Another matter that tended to upset the domestic harmony from time to time was the fact that Mr and Mrs Carew had the defects of their qualities. They were, if anything, both too popular. If Walter Carew was a 'ladies' man', Edith Carew was very much a 'man's woman'. She liked admiration, and she got a great deal of it. Conspicuous among her friends of the opposite sex was a certain Mr Henry Dickinson, a young bank-clerk who had charge of the ledger in which her account was kept. The intimacy had begun in a platonic enough fashion, and, so far as Mrs Carew was concerned, it would probably have stopped there. But this was not enough for the other, and, finding her reception of his overtures not altogether unresponsive, he proceeded from finance to romance.

After a time, young Dickinson formed the impression, from the hints and half-confidences she gave him, that Edith Carew was ill-treated or at any rate 'misunderstood' by her husband. The thought filled him with fury. The pathetic face and pleading voice of the woman he had admired beyond all others kept coming between himself and his work. He began to write to her warm, ardent letters, full of devotion and a desire to be of service. Their recipient tore them up, and threw them into her waste-paper basket.

It was an action that brought unexpected and tragic consequences.

Although he did not know how far it had gone, Walter Carew was quite aware of the young clerk's intimacy with his wife. But he appeared to look upon it from a tolerant standpoint. At any rate, he did nothing to stop it. Perhaps he thought that his wife was entitled to 'have her fling'. He had had one himself. This was connected with a Miss Annie Luke, a girl with whom, years earlier, he had had an 'understanding' in his bachelor days. He had, however, not attempted to conceal this intimacy from his wife; and she, for her part, had always affected to regard it as of no consequence. As she said, when they discussed the matter, the Annie Luke episode had come to nothing; the woman had gone out of her husband's life, and, since his marriage, they had never met or corresponded.

Yet the shadow of Annie Luke was responsible for the tragedy that was to follow.

It was in the autumn of 1896 that the long-forgotten name of Annie Luke first cropped up in Yokohama. One evening Mrs Carew went down to the club, and casually remarked to her husband that a woman had called that afternoon and enquired for him.

'She didn't give her name,' she said, 'and all I saw of her was that she was heavily veiled and dressed in black.'

'A "Woman in Black",' said Carew reflectively. 'It sounds mysterious. Did she leave any message?'

'No, but she left a card for you. It has nothing on it except some initials.'

'What initials?'

'"A.L."'

Walter Carew felt vaguely disturbed at the announcement. 'A.L.' could be nobody but Annie Luke. They had not met for years. What on earth did she want with him now? And why had she come to Japan after this long interval? Also, why had she not left an address at which he could get in touch with her?

A couple of days passed without anything more happening. Then he was told by his wife that the 'Woman in Black' had paid another call during his absence, and had left a second card for him. This one merely had scribbled on it 'M.J. and A.L.'

The puzzle had increased. 'A.L.', of course, was Annie Luke. But who on earth was 'M.J.'? The only person he could think of with such initials was Mary Jacob, his children's governess and an inmate of his household. Therefore, these initials must belong to somebody else.

He was still puzzling over the card, and wondering what it meant, when a letter was delivered to him at the club:

107

I *must* see you. Why have you done nothing since you got my two cards? Or perhaps she never let you get them. I cannot meet her again. She makes me mad when I think of what I might have done for you. I cannot give you any address. I am living wherever I can find shelter; but you can find me and help me if you will, as I know you will for the sake of old times.

*Annie*

On the off-chance of getting in touch with her, Walter Carew went round to the shipping offices and enquired if any such person had arrived or left. As her name was not on any of the passenger-lists, he addressed a letter to Miss Luke at the *poste-restante*:

I feel greatly upset about you, and, ever since I got your card last Saturday, I have been endeavouring to find you. I wish to, and will, help you if I can only find you. Meet me this evening at 5.30 p.m. on the Bund, opposite the Club Hotel.

*W*

The appointment was not kept. Nor did Carew ever know if his message had been received, for the next day he felt ill and stopped in bed.

From the first, Mrs Carew did all that could be expected of a devoted and anxious wife. Thus, although her husband declared that he was suffering from nothing more than a bilious attack or a touch of the sun, she insisted on sending for a medical man, Dr Wheeler. By him the case was diagnosed as stomachic inflammation, and a simple remedy was prescribed. It appeared to be beneficial in its results. Suddenly, however, there was a relapse. Dr Wheeler felt so disturbed that he called in a brother practitioner, and had the patient taken to hospital. Within a couple of hours of his admission, Walter Carew was dead.

All the members of the British community at Yoko-hama were deeply shocked when they heard of Walter Carew's death. They were, however, soon to have a still greater shock. This was caused by the action of Dr Wheeler in going to the coroner[1] and demanding that a post-mortem should be conducted.

Although he recognised he was running counter to popular opinion, which held that he was causing the widow unnecessary distress, Dr Wheeler felt that he had very good grounds for withholding a certificate. He had not mentioned it to anyone, except the coroner, but a dreadful suspicion had been disturbing him ever since the patient's relapse. What, however, specially disturbed him was that a mysterious note, reading, 'Three bottles of arsenic in one week – Maruya', had been pushed under his door. As Maruya was the name of a Japanese chemist in Yokohama, he had gone there and examined the entries in the poisons-book. He was astonished to discover that this firm had supplied Mrs Carew with a considerable quantity of arsenic.

Enquiries in other directions elicited the fact that this purchase of arsenic was known to Miss Jacob, the governess. Miss Jacob had discussed the matter with a friend, Elsa Christoffel; and Elsa Christoffel had spoken about it to her employer, Mr Charles Dunlop, a leading merchant in the town. The next thing that happened was that Mr Dunlop took it upon himself to give Dr Wheeler a hint that there might be something untoward afoot.

'Of course,' he said, 'it may be nothing more than girls' gossip. Still, as poor Carew was your patient, you might care to look into it for yourself.'

'Thanks,' said the doctor, 'I mean to.'

Arsenic! Dr Wheeler began to see daylight. Various symptoms in the dead man's illness that had been puzzling him did so no longer. He went off at once to consult Mrs Carew. In answer to his questions, she told him quite

[1]EDITOR'S NOTE The coroner was a member of Her Britannic Majesty's Consulate in Yokohama. Another account of the case (in *Noted Murder Mysteries* by Philip Curtin [a pen-name of Mrs Belloc Lowndes]; Simpkin, Marshall, Hamilton, Kent & Co., London 1914) notes 'that between two and three years later, Japan was fully admitted to the comity of nations, and the foreign Consular jurisdiction was abolished'.

frankly that her husband had been treating himself with arsenic for a complaint that he had kept private.

'Why didn't you tell me of this when you first sent for me?'

'I'm afraid it didn't occur to me. Poor Walter's illness drove everything else out of my head.'

But it put something into her visitor's head, and he went off to see Mr Carey Hall, the coroner. As a result of what he was told, that official ordered an inquest to be held.

Things proceeded swiftly. Walter Carew had died on 22 October, and the inquest opened two days later. Mrs Carew, dressed in deep mourning and accompanied by one of her friends, Mr Lowder, a barrister, was obviously much affected. Everybody was full of sympathy for her and her tragically sudden widowhood.

Important medical evidence was given by Dr Wheeler. Mr Carew's symptoms, he said, had made him suspect poisoning, and it was on this account that he had had him removed to hospital. He could not, however, state the actual cause of death unless a post-mortem were held. The next witness, Miss Jacob, had something very odd to tell the coroner. This was that when she called at the shop of Maruya to get some arsenic for Mrs Carew, the assistant there had said to her, 'Why so plenty much deadly poison wanted in your house?' On being questioned as to this, Mrs Carew said that her husband had, for some years past, been in the habit of taking arsenic to relieve attacks of liver congestion, and that she had purchased it quite openly.

Much against his will, for he had naturally wished to keep in the background, Mrs Carew's friend, Henry Dickinson, had been summoned by the coroner. His evidence was unimportant except in two particulars. One was that the dead man had told him that he took arsenic; and the other was that he himself had noticed a 'veiled woman, dressed in black', hovering about the club on the day that the person said to be Annie Luke had enquired for Walter Carew. He had not seen her since. Nor could

110

he give a description of her appearance.

'Did your husband ever speak to you of anybody called Annie Luke?' Mrs Carew was asked.

'Yes,' was the reply. 'He told me all about her. Shortly before his death, he said that he wished to make amends to her.'

As everything centred round Annie Luke, a number of questions respecting this mysterious individual were put to Mrs Carew. Her story was an odd one. On 10 October, she said, while her husband was at the club, a strange woman called and enquired for him.

'What sort of a woman?' demanded a member of the jury.

'I could only see that she was tall and heavily veiled.'

'Did you tell your husband?'

'I sent a note down to him at once. I also went to the club myself, and discussed it with him there. He was very puzzled, as he understood she was still in England.'

On the coroner's suggestion, Mrs Carew's note was read to the jury:

*Dearest Walter*, – A most mysterious lady (?) came here just now and asked to see Mr Walter Carew. I told her you were not in, when she said she would call again early this evening, about 4.30, as she *must* see you. She would give no name, nor any reason for her visit. . . . Will you be back to see your 'Woman in Black'? If not, what message shall I tell Rachel to give her? Enclosed is her card.

Yours,
Edith

The atmosphere of Yokohama seemed strangely full of anonymous letters, all purporting to have come from Miss Luke. First of all, there was the one to Mr Carew; then, after his death, there were others to Mrs Carew; and, finally, both Mr Lowder and Mr Hall had received similar missives. Those addressed to Mrs Carew read as follows:

111

Beware! Dare to speak one word of the truth, and you shall never leave Japan alive.

and:

I have done what I can for you. True, I have made you suffer, but I have written to Mr Hall and to Mr Lowder. Yokohama will be troubled no more by A.L.

The communication sent to Mr Lowder was still more mysterious in tone:

I do not know you, but I gather from Saturday's papers that you are acting on behalf of the wife of the man who was to me the world, and more than the world.

Dead men tell no tales; no, nor dead women either, for I am going to join him. Do you know what waiting means for eight long weary years? I have watched and waited. Waited till I knew he would grow tired of her, that silly little fool. And then I came to him. What is the result? We, between us, electrify Japan.

I have never pretended to be a good woman; but, for the sake of a few lines, I do not see why I should let a silly innocent woman be condemned for what she knows nothing about. . . .

By the time you get this I shall be well on my way to join him, my twin soul. . . . I shall write to the coroner.

A.L.

The letter to the coroner was equally hysterical. If it meant anything, it meant that the writer contemplated suicide:

Mr Hall – I have finished a letter to Mr Lowder, so cannot begin this to you in quite the same way. Shall I begin with the truest and wisest saying on this earth, 'Woman is at the bottom of everything.' In this case it is so, for, between us, we have bamboozled the lot of you: (1) the chemist, (2) the doctor, and last, but not least, that fool his wife.

112

I shall stop here, because my last act on earth shall be a merciful one, and because I am going to join him, my twin soul. I will exonerate the little fool from any share in helping us to meet each other. I have done my work well, and I am taking good care to escape the lot of you and the law.

. . . The world will call me mad; I am, however, sane enough to know what I have done, and what I am going to do; and sane enough to accomplish my end – that as we were divided in life, we were not in death. I wonder whether, out of all this community, there is one who can sympathise with me who goes out to meet her Maker.

*A.L.*

After this evidence had been given, the coroner adjourned the enquiry, and directed Dr Divers, Professor of Chemistry at the University of Tokyo, to make an analysis of certain of the dead man's organs. The result, which was awaited with profound interest, read as follows:

I have come to the definite conclusion that the deceased died from the effects of arsenic, which was administered to him without his knowledge.

While they now knew the cause of Walter Carew's death, the jury had still to discover who had been responsible for it. The anonymous letters, of course, pointed to this individual being Annie Luke. It seemed beyond question. The coroner, however, in his summing-up, made it clear that he had very strong doubts if such a woman even existed in Japan. Mrs Carew, he reminded them, had said she had seen her on 10 October. After that date, however, she had disappeared, and the most diligent search had failed to establish any trace of her. Yet on 29 October she had written to himself and to Mr Lowder the letters they had heard read. Where, then, was she during the interval? Whoever it was that had administered arsenic to Walter Carew, he could not advise the jury to find that it was Annie Luke. With regard, however, to Mrs Carew, there was no getting over the fact that she had obtained a quantity of arsenic from Maruya's shop. It had not been ordered by a doctor. Why, then, did she want it?

The problem before the jury was a difficult one. As the simplest way out of it, they returned an 'open verdict'. The deceased, they said, had died from arsenical poisoning, but there was 'no direct evidence to show by whom it had been administered'. This, of course, was an improper finding, for their verdict should have been based on the inadequacy, and not on the alleged 'indirectness', of the evidence offered them.

Public opinion in Yokohama was very much against Mr Coroner Hall; it was felt that he had acted with bias. All the sympathy was with Mrs Carew, who had become a widow under such tragic circumstances. It was freely recognised, however, that the mystery of her husband's death would not be solved until Annie Luke was found. Mrs Carew herself was so strongly of that opinion that she offered a substantial reward for her discovery, and inserted an advertisement to that effect in the local papers.

'Only find this woman for me,' she said wistfully, 'and you will find poor Walter's murderer.'

There were plenty of volunteers to join in the hunt. All day long, eager enquiries were made at hotels, boarding-houses, hospitals, and shipping and tourist and railway offices. But a blank was drawn everywhere. Nobody had seen such a person as Annie Luke arrive; nobody had seen her leave. This, of course, was odd, for the number of Englishwomen in the town was not so large that a stranger among them could come and go without attracting attention.

But the search did have one result. This took the form of another anonymous letter received by Mr Lowder:

It never occurred to you, did it, that 'my way' to join *him* might be by the French mail? It never occurred to you, did it, that I can disguise myself as well as my name? It never occurred to you, did it, that you never could, and never would, find me? Who am I, and what is my name, eh? Is it 'A.L.', or 'M.J.', or was I, during my stay in Yokohama, passing under some other name, eh?

*A.L.*

Just a week after the coroner's inquiry had been held, Yokohama was to have a fresh sensation. This was the arrest of Edith Carew on a charge of wilful murder.

The authorities lost no time in setting the scene for the second act of the drama. A couple of days after her arrest, Edith Carew was confronting Mr James Troup, Assistant Judge of the Consular Court. At this investigation she had the services of two members of the local Bar, Mr J.F. Lowder and Mr A.B. Walford, while Mr H.C. Litchfield, the Public Prosecutor, presented the case for the Crown.

The first witnesses called by Mr Litchfield were Mary Jacob and Elsa Christoffel. Miss Jacob, it transpired, had not been on good terms with Mrs Carew, and was under notice to leave her employment just before the tragedy. Considering that some of her letters from England were being improperly withheld, she had examined a waste-paper basket in one of the rooms. There she had found a number of torn-up scraps. Struck by their appearance, she took them to her friend, Miss Christoffel, who had stitched the fragments together.

'Why did you do that?' Miss Christoffel was asked.

'Because I thought it would be useful to my friend's character, if anything were ever said against it. The letters I put together would show that men were in the habit of paying visits to the house, and that these visits were not to Miss Jacob.'

What Dr Wheeler had to say was a repetition of what he had already said at the coroner's inquest. In cross-examination, he admitted that Mrs Carew had exhibited much anxiety about her husband's symptoms, and had readily agreed that a second doctor should be consulted.

'What did she say,' he was asked, 'when you told her that you were removing her husband to hospital?'

'She said, "Do you think it necessary?"'

Henry Dickinson was subjected to a very bad hour in the witness-box, for he had to listen to the letters he had written to Mrs Carew being read in public. Some of them made it clear that he had been on terms of remarkably close intimacy with her.

I cannot go to bed, my sweet, without writing a line which I shall deliver if I can before I go down. . . . My poor, dear darling. I knew you would suffer for yesterday, but it is revealed to me more than ever, dearest, how much I love you, and how much you have become to me. . . . I love you utterly, my dear one, and the remembrance of yesterday will ever be with me.

My poor dear darling. I knew you would suffer for yesterday. I shall always hope that all this constant abuse of me will never cause you to look at me with other eyes than those you have now.

A second ran:

You ask me, dearest, to take time over answering your letter, and, in the same breath, to give it you at tiffin. . . . It is impossible to go back to the old footing. *He* has altered all that; and, if you were a free woman, I would ask you to come to me. You know this. Long ago, when I first knew you, something of a passion for you would now and then come over me, and envy of the man who had *you*; and now, when you are thoroughly estranged and have come to me for help, what I had easily checked before has risen again with a strength that is multiplied a thousandfold by the knowledge that now you love me.

Dearest, the scene of last night shall not take place again. We cannot help now, I think, loving. I know it is wrong, but you are not to blame, I think, so much as I, but for other sakes than ours the grosser sin shall be avoided.

116

There were also guarded references to the mysterious Annie Luke:

I have been thinking about your probably having to meet this woman. I wish for your sake that you could refuse to, but have come to think that you cannot well do so. Do you know anything against her? If not, you should meet her, I think.

A sensational occurrence marked this preliminary hearing. When the letters that had been put in as exhibits were being gathered together, one of them could not be found. There-upon, the judge directed that the doors should be locked, and everybody set to work to look for the missing document. Mrs Carew, who was sitting beside her counsel, also joined in the hunt. But it seemed to have vanished into thin air. During the adjournment for luncheon, a police matron was instructed to search Mrs Carew. The result was that the letter was discovered hidden in her coat-cuff. When this was reported to her junior counsel, Mr Walford, he returned his brief; and the whole conduct of the defence was taken over by Mr Lowder. Thereupon, Mr Litchfield, the Crown Prosecutor, asked that she should be committed for trial by a jury. This course was adopted; and Mrs Carew, who had hitherto been on bail, was transferred in custody to the consular prison.

While, of course, indefensible, the reason for Mrs Carew's anxiety to suppress this particular letter from Mr Dickinson was not unnatural. It was declared to be 'such as no modest woman who still retained fealty to her husband could accept'.

The trial was held in the Supreme Court at Yokohama, before Mr Justice Mowat and a jury. Mrs Carew, still dressed in deep mourning, and accompanied by her brother and a prison matron, drove up in a jinricksha.

The indictment ran as follows:

117

In her Britannic Majesty's Court for Japan, Kanagawa to wit, the 5th day of January, 1897. Henry Charles Litchfield, the Crown Prosecutor in Japan for Our Lady the Queen, presents and charges that at Yokohama, Japan, Edith May Hallowell Carew on the 22nd day of October in the Year of Our Lord 1896 feloniously, wilfully, and of malice aforethought did kill and murder one Walter Raymond Hallowell Carew against the peace of Our Lady the Queen, her Crown and Dignity.

There was a moment's pause. Then the question was put to the prisoner:

'How say you, Edith May Hallowell Carew, are you guilty or not guilty?'

'I am not guilty,' answered the accused woman in a voice that was scarcely heard.

The plea having been entered, the names of the jurors were called. Although only five were required, considerable difficulty was found in assembling this number. Nine of those on the list did not answer their names; three others put in a medical certificate of ill health; two declared that they should be exempted on the grounds of deafness; four were challenged.

Given motive and opportunity in one and the same person, it is not difficult to establish a strong presumption of guilt. Undoubtedly such presumption existed so far as Edith Carew was concerned. Her illicit 'friendship' with the young bank clerk supplied the motive for accomplishing Walter Carew's death; and the fact that she had nursed him in his last illness supplied the opportunity.

Mr Wilkinson, of the Shanghai Bar, who opened the case for the Crown, admitted that practically all the evidence he would offer was circumstantial. The law, he said, did not require that there should be any actual witnesses; if it did, a conviction could never be secured in a case of suspected poisoning. But, apart from circumstantial evidence, he had direct evidence that Mrs Carew had bought a quantity of arsenic, and that, in her

118

relations with Mr Dickinson, she had a demonstrable motive for causing the death of her husband.

The witness who aroused the most interest was Henry Dickinson. His position was an unhappy one, as he again had to give evidence against the woman with whom he had had a 'romance', and also to endure the ordeal of having his love-letters read to a gaping and curious public.

Among those letters was one which indicated something remarkably akin to a conspiracy between himself and its recipient:

It will be necessary to be quite in accord with each other. On broad questions, we must be able to answer alike. You first wrote to me about the money – writing to the man you could best entrust with some of your own unhappiness.

Money was a necessity; and it was a very natural thing to come to me about it. This, of course, led to my advising you how to get it; and, as the money proved a source of much anxiety to yourself on account of his attempts to get it, I often saw you at your house.

If ever questioned *re* meeting me on the Hills, we must admit it, of course, as our meetings were for the purpose of talking generally over what was the best course to take as regards yourself. We met on no particular hills, mind, and never mention the fortification. It is too near the cottage, and, if possible, that should be kept out of it. We sometimes rode and sometimes walked, but our hill meetings have been so infrequent that it should be difficult to make any point against you. Our meeting-places for the one or two occasions when we did meet must be the tea-house near the steep hill, or by the race-course. . . . Burn all this, when you have read and learnt the early part.

An odd letter for a bank clerk to write. But it went on in a still odder strain, for it definitely suggested that Mrs Carew should consult a solicitor as to the possibility of securing a divorce:

119

. . . It is quite clear to me now – at all risks, at hazards – divorce. You must not mind your poor brother's and father's feelings over the scandal. Your personal safety is of more importance to us all than any scandals. . . . Now and always I will help you in all things, if you want me, and I know you do. Keep up your heart, my dear one, and do not give in under his cruelty and coarseness.

This attack on the dead man's reputation was not permitted to pass unquestioned.

'Did you yourself ever see Mr Carew treating his wife unkindly?' the witness was asked.

'Never,' was the answer. 'I know now,' he added, 'that what she told me about this was incorrect.'

This was obvious, for it was shown that, even while she was complaining of his alleged ill-treatment, Mrs Carew was writing affectionate letters to her husband. One of them began, 'My own darling', and they all ended, 'Your ever-loving wife'.

But counsel had not yet done with Mr Dickinson.

'If a divorce had been granted,' he said, 'would you have married Mrs Carew?'

'We never discussed such a step.'

The Crown Prosecutor turned to another item in the correspondence:

I should think you ought to ask for the letters. I should do so without hesitation. If I see the usual signal, I could also look in after tiffin, perhaps, though I am not certain *re* this. I should go and ask for the letters, taking care, however, no strangers are near you.

'What were these letters?' Mr Wilkinson asked.

'They were letters which Mrs Carew told me her husband had written to someone at the post office.'

'And what was the "usual signal", to which you refer?'

'That was a handkerchief which Mrs Carew would hang out of a certain window when I could go in and see her.'

A lady's handkerchief as a love-signal! The jury whispered among themselves. Even the judge looked astonished, as he recorded the fact on his notes.

Mr Dickinson, more careful than Mrs Carew, had only kept one letter from her:

> Forgive me, my dear. I always come to you in my troubles. There is nothing much the matter, but I should like your advice on a matter which must be decided early tomorrow. He is so far quite indifferent as to yesterday, beyond calling you a few inelegant names.

Evidence concerning the torn-up scraps recovered from Mrs Carew's waste-paper basket was given by Elsa Christoffel. As before, she declared that her intention had been to 'protect the character of Miss Jacob'.

'Protect it from what?' enquired Mr Lowder, cross-examining.

'Well, if it became generally known that men were visiting the house, it might be thought that they had gone there to see my friend, Miss Jacob. These letters prove the contrary.'

'And did her character require such protection?'

'No, it didn't.'

As Miss Christoffel was of Swiss birth, the judge, looking puzzled, suggested that perhaps she had not understood the question. Accepting this view, Mr Lowder went on to another point, and extracted from her a statement that she had written an anonymous letter. This she had sent to a man who visited at the Carews' house, and was to warn him not to go there again. 'Call this the product of a mad woman,' it said, 'but keep away from that house.'

Elsa Christoffel had also written the word 'Maruya' on the slip of paper that led Dr Wheeler to discover where Mrs Carew had purchased arsenic.

'It was the name of the Japanese chemist,' she explained. 'I heard of it from Miss Jacob, and I wrote it down at the request of my employer, Mr Dunlop.'

The case was full of surprises. In the middle of the proceedings, Mr Lowder adopted a very odd course. As it seemed obvious that Walter Carew's death had resulted from arsenical poisoning not administered by himself, he could only clear his client by establishing that somebody else had administered it. For this purpose, he fixed on Mary Jacob, and, in his capacity as a 'private individual', he had her arrested and charged with the murder.

This second case proceeded concurrently with that of Mrs Carew, but was heard in the Consular Court before Mr Troup, the Assistant Judge. There was much public sympathy for Miss Jacob, and a subscription was set on foot to secure legal help. This was supplied by Mr George Scidmore, Deputy Consul for America.

Although Mr Lowder protested that he brought the charge from a 'sense of duty', his action was much criticised. What he endeavoured to establish was that the 'Annie Luke' letters were really written by Miss Jacob. In one of them the expression 'twin soul' occurred. It also occurred in a novel by Marie Corelli. Miss Jacob was fond of reading novels by this author. Consequently, she had written the letters.

This was not regarded by the court as a very brilliant piece of deduction. When the judge said so, Mr Lowder began a fresh attack, and suggested that questionable relations had existed between Miss Jacob and Walter Carew. As he was no more successful in this, he declared that he would offer further evidence at the next hearing. But, during the interval, he altered his mind; letting the matter drop, he returned to the defence of Mrs Carew.

Public interest in the case was such that long reports were telegraphed to England at the end of each day's hearing. The majority of these accounts were quite reliable. Some odd influences, however, were at work, for, in the middle of the proceedings, a London journal printed a message 'From Our Own Correspondent', purporting to give the result:

The Carew murder trial at Yokohama has collapsed in dramatic fashion. Miss Jacob has confessed to the poisoning of Mr Carew and to the authorship of the mysterious letters.

This, of course, was at once denied by the responsible agencies. A reward of 500 dollars was also offered for information as to the sender of the telegram. There were whispers of 'Annie Luke', but nothing definite ever transpired.

There was a long battle of words as to the authorship of the letters signed 'A.L'. As this was held to be the key to the mystery, it involved much argument. Mr William Mason, an English master at Tokyo, who was put forward by the Crown as an expert, declared that the handwriting in all of the letters resembled that of Mrs Carew, and not, as the defence had alleged, that of either Miss Jacob or Miss Christoffel.

Mr Lowder would give way on one point only. This was the contention that a letter, with the signature 'A.L. Price', which had been sent to Sir Ernest Satow, H.B.M.'s Minister at Tokyo, had been written by Mrs Carew.

'She wrote it,' he said, 'in a fit of distraction and while smarting under a sense of the injustice done her by the coroner. It was natural she should have sought redress from her own Minister. If she had put her own name to it, no fault would have been found with her.'

Sir Ernest Satow himself gave evidence that he had received this letter, which ran as follows:

*Dear Sir*, – I wish to call your attention to the very scandalous way in which our Consul, Mr Hall, has conducted the inquest on the late Mr Carew. Had he any right to sum up in the face of the evidence produced as he has done?

*Faithfully yours,*
*A.L. Price.*

For hour after hour, and day after day, the racked woman sat in the dreadful shadow of the dock, listening with strained attention to the pleadings of the counsel on either side. One side battling for her freedom; the other for her conviction. Hope alternated with despair. Perhaps the worst ordeal to which she was subjected was having to listen to the Dickinson letters being read to the jury. Henry Dickinson was her friend. What could have possessed him to write such letters? What, however, was much more to the point was why had she not burned them to ashes, and destroyed them utterly? Mr Lowder affected to regard them as of small consequence, protesting that a young man in love would write anything, and imagine encouragement where it did not exist. But it was clear that the jury were unconvinced. They had been young themselves.

Owing to the number of adjournments, the case dragged on for nearly a month. It was not until 1 February, more than three weeks after the hearing commenced, that Mr Lowder was able to address the jury. This address was of more length than strength. Much of it was occupied with an attempt to discredit Mary Jacob and Elsa Christoffel. Referring to them as a 'couple of pilfering thieves', counsel suggested that they had improperly endeavoured to throw suspicion on his client. As for the 'Annie Luke' letters, he still held that Edith Carew could not have written them, because they contained expressions unlike any she would have employed. The Dickinson correspondence, he said, had been put forward to establish that the prisoner had a motive for accomplishing her husband's death. 'Yet no woman,' he declared, 'ever had a more complaisant husband. Why should this one want to be free of a husband who gave her every facility for indulging in flirtations? If Mrs Carew wrote of him as bullying her, it was merely an exaggerated method of attracting the sympathetic interest of Henry Dickinson, with whom she was for the moment amusing herself.'

In support of his rather odd theories, Mr Lowder quoted the Latin epigram: *Quid levius penna? Pulvis. Quid pulvere? Ventus. Quid vento? Mulier. Quid muliere? Nihil.*

For the benefit of those of his hearers who had not kept up their classics, he supplied a rough and ready rendering, and declared that the Dickinson episode was simply a 'passing flirtation'. 'If,' he added, 'Mrs Carew permitted this witness a greater degree of encouragement than was strictly prudent, she did no more than hundreds of women have done before her, and will continue to do despite anything that moralists may preach to the contrary.'

Warned, apparently, by the expressions on the faces of the married members of the jury that this was a dangerous line to follow, he dropped it and took up another one. This was that Mrs Carew had so little motive for causing her husband's death that, when it occurred, she was arranging to buy him a partnership in a silk business. He then went on to discuss whether Walter Carew had died from poisoning at all; and, if so, whether it had been administered by himself or by somebody else. The post-mortem, he remarked, had revealed the presence of three distinct poisons in the dead man's body, but only one of them had been purchased by Mrs Carew. Moreover, she had purchased it quite openly, and at the request of her husband. 'An affectionate wife and mother,' he said solemnly, 'does not turn all at once and by easy stages into the dreadful wickedness of a Borgia.'

The peroration ended on a high note:

'Confronted, gentlemen, with this monstrous charge of murder, my client has stood erect, proudly assured of her innocence. Her courage has never failed her. Gentlemen, I am cheered by the reflection that, however wanting the defence set up may be, a prisoner in the position of my client is never unprotected in a court of law that is presided over by a British judge, assisted by a British jury!'

The Crown Prosecutor followed with a speech that, although it took a long time to do so, made short work of much that the defence had said. When he had finished with a solemn injunction to the jury to deliver a verdict 'in accordance with the facts, and irrespective of their feelings,' the judge delivered his charge.

The summing-up of Mr Justice Mowat was eminently fair. Still, he, like the coroner, let it be seen that he had grave doubts as to the corporate existence (at any rate in Japan) of the mysterious Annie Luke. As for the letters purporting to have been written by her, it was, he said, difficult to make satisfactory deductions from them. With regard, however, to the Dickinson letters, they at least showed that Mrs Carew had appealed to the writer for sympathy by representing that her marital relations were unhappy. Yet her own counsel had protested that they were quite happy. The prosecution, not accepting this, had suggested that the letters written by Mr Dickinson, which were obviously a response to those written to him, furnished a motive for the crime. Not, of course, that a motive was necessary. Still, it was a help in solving such a problem as the one that now had to be solved – that is, by whose hand had Walter Carew been sent to his death?

'I ask you, gentlemen,' were the judge's last words, 'to consider your verdict. It must not be based on suspicion, however strong, or on conjecture, however probable. It must be based on conviction that is founded on the evidence, and on nothing else. You must do your duty honestly and fearlessly.'

Thus directed, the jury withdrew, to discuss the strange and tragic story to which they had been listening for twenty-one days. It was thought that they would be absent for a long period. Yet within half an hour a message was received from the foreman that they had come to a decision.

'Are you agreed upon your verdict?' enquired the Clerk of the Court, when they had filed back into their places.

'We are,' answered the foreman.

'How say you, is the prisoner at the bar guilty or not guilty?'

'Guilty.'

'And is that the verdict of you all?'

'It is.'

'Edith May Hallowell Carew,' said the clerk, turning to the trembling woman in the dock. 'Have you anything to say why sentence should not be passed?'

126

'No,' she whispered.

A tense hush settled upon the court. 'The face of the accused,' says an eye-witness, 'became overspread with a ghastly dull tint; the lines of her lips slackened; the look of a stricken animal crept into her eyes; and her hands clutched convulsively at the ledge of the dock.'

Suddenly there was a stir as Mr Justice Mowat was seen to be placing a small square of black silk upon his wig.

'Edith May Hallowell Carew,' he said in a solemn voice, 'the sentence of the court is that you forthwith be taken from where you now stand to the British Consular Jail at Yokohama. There you will remain interned until, on a day to be appointed by the proper authority, you shall be led out to the place of your execution within the precincts of the Consular Jail, and there you shall be hanged by the neck until you are dead; and your body shall then be taken down and buried with the precincts of the jail; and may God have mercy on your soul.'

The conviction of Edith Carew automatically resulted in the collapse of the charge against Mary Jacob. As a matter of fact, Mr Lowder himself withdrew it voluntarily, and before the verdict had been delivered. Thereupon, she was given the following certificate:

A charge by a private prosecutor was laid in H.B.M.'s Court here on January 10th, 1897, against Mary Esther Jacob of having murdered one Walter Hallowell Carew at this place.

A preliminary examination in the case was held before me, as Assistant Judge of the Court, on various subsequent dates; and on this 5th day of February application was made by the Prosecutor for permission to withdraw the charge. This permission was granted by the Court, and no imputation whatever in connection with this matter rests on Mary Esther Jacob.

*James Troup*.
H.B.M's Consul, British Consulate, Yokohama.

Miss Jacob also received the following letter from Mr Lowder himself:

*February 13th, 1897.*
*Madame*, – I am this moment, and for the first time, in receipt of proof which is conclusive to my mind that you were not the writer of the 'A.L.' letters; and I now hasten to ask you to accept that apology which I have heretofore been unable conscientiously to offer you for the pain and mental suffering to which you have been put in consequence of the charge I considered it my duty to prefer against you, and which I am now convinced was unfounded.

*Very faithfully,*
*J.F. Lowder.*

This was all very well, so far as it went. As, however, it did not go far enough, Miss Jacob's legal adviser asked for a more detailed disclaimer. What he particularly wanted was a withdrawal of the offensive suggestion that an improper measure of intimacy had existed between Miss Jacob and Mr Carew. The withdrawal was promptly supplied:

*Sir*, – the publication of the letter addressed to Miss Jacob (on the 13th inst.) has resulted in the communication to me of facts which indicate the existence of a depth of duplicity and deceit which is to my mind unimaginable; of which I, among others, have been the unconscious dupe, and Miss Jacob the victim. . . . Words fail me to express the regret with which the hearing of the story has filled me; for I feel that an act of injustice has been committed, for which, had it been intentional on my part, no reparation in my power could be adequate.
. . . Believe me, my single desire and sole concern is to satisfy your client by doing what lies in my power to restore her character to the extent that I have been instrumental in impeaching it; and, to that end, I now explicitly withdraw every word I have said imputing

the existence of questionable relations between her and the late Mr Carew.

An advocate should, of course, be zealous in the defence of his client. Still, there is such a thing as pressing this beyond justifiable limits. It was certainly felt that Mr Lowder had done so in impeaching the character of Miss Jacob, by first charging her with murdering Mr Carew, and then with having committed misconduct with him.

So far as the public were concerned, this was the end of the 'Carew Case'. But it was not an altogether satisfactory end. The trial had left many problems still unsolved. They never were solved. It is clear, however, that the author of the 'Annie Luke' letters was either the actual poisoner of Walter Carew or somebody in close touch with that individual. Who, then, wrote those letters? If not Mrs Carew, it must have been somebody who had come to Yokohama for the express purpose of murdering Walter Carew. The defence had suggested that his slayer was Annie Luke. Yet nobody but Mrs Carew had seen her in Japan. Nor was anything ever seen of her afterwards in England.

Wilkie Collins created a 'Woman in White'. Did Edith Carew create a 'Woman in Black'?

Edith Carew was spared the last shame of the scaffold. Exercising the prerogative of mercy that, as British Minister in Japan, was vested in him, Sir Ernest Satow commuted the death sentence to one of penal servitude for life.

# The Girl With the Golden Hair
*Frank M. O'Brien*

Some historical society concerned with the social past of
Brooklyn may yet put a bronze tablet at the corner of
Bedford Avenue and Hancock Street to indicate that
there, in the earliest years of the twentieth century,
was the stamping ground of the Bedford Gang. The
young men who made up this odorous coterie were not
budding burglars or even gregarious gunmen. Most of
them worked as clerks six days of the week. The rest
had rich fathers or indulgent mothers. The youths dressed
flashily, wore their hats cocked well back on their heads,
knew the slang of the day to the last syllable, and usually
had money in their pockets.

They ornamented this particular corner, which is two
short blocks north of Fulton Street,[1] almost every evening, and always, unless it rained, they were there on
Sunday afternoons. Sunday was the particular day for
their avocation, which was the hunting of women. Every
girl who came past the corner was subjected to a fusillade
of their peculiar wit. If she fled, they snickered and
practised jig steps until the next one came along. If she
decided to linger and trade conversation with them, so
much the better for them and the worse for her. Unlike
four-footed predatory beasts, they did not quarrel over
their prey, but were, as a rule, communistic.

The chief of the Bedford Gang in 1901 was, by

[1] EDITOR'S NOTE: A major street running east from near the Brooklyn
Bridge.

common acclaim, Handsome Harry Casey. It was he who introduced Florence Burns to Walter Brooks in the spring of that year. It must be said for Harry Casey that, when the time came for an enquiry into the past of Florence Burns, he went forward to say that, from all he knew of her, she was a good girl. This may not be considered a great act of chivalry, but in the unwritten history of the Bedford Gang it stands alone. The gang was not in the habit of saying kind things about women, or even to women.

Walter Brooks was twenty years old, and Florence Burns was nineteen. He lived with his parents in Decatur Street, only a few blocks from the Bedford Gang's corner, and was in the produce commission business in Jay Street, Manhattan. Florence Burns was a tall, handsome girl, with hair that was really golden. She lived with her parents in the Flatbush part of Brooklyn. They were not rich, but they were distinctly respectable.

There is no doubt but that at one time Walter Brooks was in love with Florence Burns and intended to marry her. He introduced her to his mother at a dinner in a Manhattan hotel in October 1901, and on 3 November the girl dined by invitation at the Brooks' home. On the Sunday after that, the couple went to church together and returned to Walter's home for dinner. Young Brooks had given up his place among the Bedford Gang.

Late in November of the same year, Walter Brooks brought Florence Burns to his home and turned her over to his mother's care. The girl was ill. The boy told his parents that Florence had been put out of her own home. There had been a quarrel, he understood, because the Burnses objected to their daughter's constant companionship with him.

While Florence Burns was recovering at the Brooks' home, the young man's parents heard things which led them to believe that the relations between him and Florence had not been such as they could approve.

'What are you going to do?' Mr Brooks heard Florence say to Walter early in December. 'Are you going to marry me? My health is broken and I don't know what to do.' She was crying.

Young Brooks advised her to seek employment, and said that he would do what he could to help her. Florence Burns's tone was angry when she again asserted that her health had been ruined and that she could not work.

A day or two later, young Brooks came down with a fever, and in his delirium his talk was full of his mother and with hardly a word about Florence Burns. He said over and over that he was not going to leave home. There was bitter comment from Florence Burns, and the next day she left the Brooks' home. She returned frequently to see how Walter was doing, and on almost every visit there were words between her and Mrs Brooks, who finally told the girl that she and Mr Brooks would never allow Walter to marry her.

'She replied to that,' said Mrs Brooks in telling of that incident, 'that if Walter did not marry her she would shoot him. And she added, "And if I shoot, I will shoot to kill, because both my mother and myself are good shots."'

A short time afterwards, the elder Brooks found it necessary to talk with Florence and ask her to stop 'hounding Walter', as he expressed it. He told the girl that he would never consent to Walter's marrying her, and that as Walter was under age they could not be married without his parents' consent.

That ended communication between the girl and the parents of the man she loved. But her affair with Walter Brooks continued. Whether from fondness, whether from fear, he saw nearly as much of her as he ever had. Probably it was fondness, because about the first of the year Walter Brooks took Florence Burns to a church in McDonough Street, Brooklyn, where he had gone to Sunday school before the days of the Bedford Gang, and asked the pastor to marry them. The pastor refused because Brooks admitted that he was not of age and that his parents would not consent to the marriage.

The fact that Florence Burns had been wasting her time and affections on a man whose parents would not let him marry her caused such friction in the girl's home that she left it and went to board at the house of a Mrs Hitchcock in West Forty-fifth Street, Manhattan. Brooks used to call on her there two or three evenings a week. They would leave the house about eight o'clock, but Florence Burns was always back at her boarding-place by midnight.

Yet all the time there was another woman in the case. This was Ruth Dunn, a girl of about Florence Burns's age. Florence had introduced Walter Brooks to her months before, and the three had been together frequently. When Florence Burns began to bore him with too much marriage talk, Brooks, who had no pleasure except in the companionship of women, began to pay attention to Ruth Dunn. When February 1902 came, Brooks saw Florence Burns about six nights a week and was with Ruth Dunn six afternoons. And Florence Burns found it out. One day Brooks told his partner, Harry Cohen, that he had seen Florence the night before and that she had repeated her demand that he marry her, and followed it up with a threat.

'If anything happens,' Cohen said Brooks remarked, 'you'll know what caused it.'

Several times during the week beginning 9 February, Florence Burns went to Brooks's office, but did not always find him there. On Thursday the 13th, she called at the office and, not finding him, left this note:

Walter, dear – Am going to Detroit tomorrow night and would like to see you before I go. Will be in again, and hope to see you. Florence.

She went to his office on Friday and, although she was told that Brooks was in Newark, she said she would wait until he returned. And she did. After a talk with her, Brooks told his partner that he would not go with him to Brooklyn, as was their custom.

'Florence is going to Detroit,' he said, 'and I've promised her a farewell dinner. I'll meet you later at the Ralph Avenue elevated station.' But this engagement was not kept. When Cohen left the office, Brooks and Florence Burns were still talking there.

The story told by Florence Burns later was that she parted from Walter Brooks at his office and never saw him again.

133

Brooks, some two hours later, entered the Glen Island Hotel, at Cortlandt and West Streets, accompanied by a woman, and registered as 'John Wilson and wife, Brooklyn'. The pair were assigned to Room 12 on the third floor. At ten o'clock the electric annunciator for Room 12 rang and a negro bellboy, George Washington by name if not by nature, answered it. The woman in Room 12 told him to bring a glass of lemon soda. Nothing more was heard from Room 12. Anthony Bolz, a policeman, who lived in the hotel and had a room directly over Brooks's and spent the evening reading, heard nothing.

About midnight, Washington went upstairs again on an errand and smelled gas as he passed the door of Room 12. He reported this to the clerk, Earle, and Earle entered Room 12, the door of which was not locked. Brooks, undressed, was lying on the bed and the room was full of gas which came from two open jets. Earle sent for a doctor, who treated Brooks for asphyxiation, injecting strychnine. Brooks seemed to be reviving and the doctor went away. He noticed a small indentation on the side of the unconscious man's head, but thought that it might have been caused by a fall. If the room had been brighter, or the doctor a little less sleepy, he might have discovered that the indentation was the place where a bullet had entered Brooks's head, just behind the right ear, to nick the brain and 'mushroom' against the opposite wall of the skull.

At six o'clock on Saturday morning, Earle went to Room 12 to see how the guest was getting on. There was a big stain on the pillow under the young man's head, and the clerk called a policeman. At the Hudson Street Hospital the wounded man was identified, from papers in his pocket, as Walter Brooks, and his parents and partner were summoned. Brooks died an hour after they arrived, without having spoken a word. Whoever killed him had made a strange stroke in turning on the gas. Even if the gas had given the alarm, it was a false alarm, and the hours in which Brooks might have spoken the name of his slayer were lost.

The dead man's father, Thomas Brooks, did not hesitate to name his suspicions to the police. They heard Cohen's story, too, and Florence Burns was arrested before noon at the home of her parents in East Fifteenth Street, Flatbush. She was calm and her story was brief. She said she had parted from Brooks at his office at 6.30 on Friday evening and had gone directly home. Finding that her parents had gone to a theatre, she went to her room, without notifying her sister Gladys of her presence, and remained there.

The police practically turned the case over to the homicide bureau of the District Attorney's office, with Assistant District Attorney Krotel in charge. It was obvious that the prime task was to prove the presence of Florence Burns at the Glen Island Hotel. The hotel clerk, Earle, had seen the woman, but could only say that she wore a black veil and dark clothes. So the investigators turned from him to the negro bellboy, George Washington. He had escorted the couple to Room 12 and he had visited the room when the woman ordered the lemon soda. He said that on the second occasion he got a good look at the woman.

According to the statement given to the newspapers by the investigators after they had questioned the bellboy, the woman in Room 12 was a 'pronounced blonde' about 5 feet 8 inches tall. Florence Burns answered this description.

Florence Burns's father retained as counsel for her Foster L. Backus, and Mr Backus started immediately to combat the tactics of the District Attorney's office, which had adopted the standard Byrnes Method[1] of questioning the prisoner. Assisted by his office mate, Frank Lord, and by a noted county detective, Eddie Reardon, Mr Krotel

[1]EDITOR'S NOTE: More generally known as the Third Degree. Superintendent Thomas F. Byrnes, one of the most corrupt members of the New York Police Department, few contemporary members of which were incorrupt, took early retirement soon after the publication in the mid-1890s of the report of an enquiry into the NYPD and its connections with the underworld and with the bosses of the Democratic Party at Tammany Hall.

tried all the tricks of the police trade on Florence Burns, but she stuck to her story that the last time she saw Brooks was hours before he registered at the Glen Island Hotel.

Backus immediately branded the bellboy's identification of his client as bogus.

'She was sitting alone in a room,' said the lawyer, 'when Washington was brought in and allowed to look at her. Then he was taken out, and he next saw her in a room with two other women. He was then told to pick out the woman he had seen at the hotel and, of course, he fell into the police trap and picked out Florence Burns. I'm going to have something to say later about that sort of thing.'

When Florence Burns was arraigned before a magistrate the next day, she was the most composed person in the room. The bellboy once more 'positively identified' her as Brooks's companion, and she was remanded to the Tombs prison, the investigators asking for a little time in which to get more evidence. The evidence they wanted was the revolver. They never found it, and nobody ever made a good guess as to where it went. Bellboys are easily amenable to police methods, but the East and North Rivers have always refused to answer questions. Whoever killed Brooks had plenty of time to slip down the narrow staircase, which was not visible to the hotel office, to Cortlandt Street: from that point the North River is only a minute's walk.

The police did find a woman's comb in Room 12, and Mrs Brooks said it was the very comb that Florence Burns wore when she was ill at the Brooks' home. It was the kind of comb, however, that might have had ten thousand duplicates in New York.

A canvass was made of all the downtown restaurants to discover where Walter Brooks ate diner that Friday evening and who was with him, but the usual supply of waiters who could remember, at a word from the police, the faces and garb of every diner they had ever seen, was lacking.

The District Attorney's office now changed its tactics,

and the D.A., Mr Jerome,[1] announced that although the case against Florence Burns seemed very strong, he would be glad if Mr Backus could present a defence that would establish the girl's innocence. If he expected that Mr Backus would step forward and assume an offensive initiative, he was much mistaken. Mr Backus was playing the ancient game of biding his time. Meanwhile, his client remained in the Tombs and combed her golden hair with a comb whose ownership permitted no dispute, it belonging to the county of New York.

Just a week after the crime, the police found a new witness, from whom great things were expected. He was Arthur G. Weible, a conductor on the Brooklyn elevated railway. His testimony was kept for a grand slam at the hearing before Justice Mayer in Special Sessions. Here, for the first time, Florence Burns was seen in grief, but her sorrow was not for herself, but because Mrs Rebecca Salome Foster, a prison philanthropist known as the Tombs Angel, had been killed in the Park Avenue Hotel fire, and Mrs Foster had been very kind to the girl in the few days they had known each other.

'I was the conductor of a train which left Brooklyn Bridge at 11.15 p.m. on 14 February [the night of the murder],' said Weible. 'Florence Burns was in the rear car. I saw her at Beverly Road station.'

This fitted in with the police theory. Beverly Road was the station nearest the Burns' home, and the hour, if Weible were to be believed, would shatter the alibi of the defence.

Next, the prosecution put forth its high card, the bellboy, George Washington. He told of showing a couple to Room 12.

'Did you get a good view of the woman?' asked Mr Jerome.

'I did,' said the bellboy. 'When I first saw her standing at the door of the parlour, I noticed that she had on a

---

[1]EDITOR'S NOTE: William Travers Jerome. One of his first cousins, *née* Jennie Jerome, was the wife of Lord Randolph Churchill; one of the Churchills' sons was named Winston.

black veil and a black, tight-fitting jacket. I noticed no
colour but black about her clothes. When I took them to
the room, she had raised her veil above her eyes and I got
a good look at her. I lighted two gas-jets and looked her
square in the face when I asked her if she wanted anything
else before leaving the room.'

'Do you see the woman here who went into Room 12
that night?' asked Mr Jerome.

'I do,' said the bellboy, pointing to Miss Burns. 'That
lady there.'

The prisoner bore his gaze unflinchingly and looked
him coolly in the face.

'Are you sure you make no mistake?'

'I'm sure she's the one. I saw her next in the police
station.'

It seemed, to those in court – barring Mr Backus
– that it was all up with Florence Burns when Mr
Jerome finished his questions. But Mr Backus had
come to the moment when there was no more time to
be bided. He examined George Washington for just five
minutes.

'While you were at the police station that day, were you
questioned about the girl?'

'Yes, by Mr Krotel from the District Attorney's office.'

'Were you asked the question, "Did you see the
woman?"'

'I was.'

'Did you stutter a little when you answered him?'

'No, sir.'

'Were you asked the question, "What did she look
like?"'

'I don't remember.'

'Didn't you answer that you were not close enough to
the girl to tell what she looked like?'

'Yes, sir,' replied the witness, as if oblivious to the
former question.

'Didn't you say to Mr Krotel that there was a woman in
the hall and that you were not close enough to her to give
a description of her?'

'Yes, sir.'

'And by that you meant the woman who was taken to Room 12?'

'Yes, sir.'

'How many persons took you from the hotel to the police station?'

'I walked along with one' – pointing out Detective Shultz.

'Had someone tried to get a description of the woman in the hotel?'

'I gave Mr Krotel a description of her.'

'Didn't you say that you were not close enough to her to give a description of her?'

'I did not.'

This was the third or fourth time the witness had contradicted himself on this point.

'Who went with you into the captain's room?'

'Does he mean when I went into the room to identify the young lady?' asked the witness of Justice Mayer.

'Then you knew what you were going in for?' broke in Mr Backus.

'Yes.'

'Did you know that this defendant was the only girl in the room?'

'I did not.'

'Describe how she looked in the captain's room.'

'She had on the same kind of hat that she had on the night before in the hotel, but she had on a different coat.'

'When you saw the defendant in the courtroom before Magistrate Cornell, did not you say that the woman in Room 12 had darker hair than the defendant?'

'I did.'

'What description did you give the police of the girl at the hotel?'

'I said I thought she had dark hair and was tall and good-looking. I told them she was not what might be called a white person.'

So, therefore, Mr Backus had established the evident fact that the only person who had seen the companion of Walter Brooks in Room No. 12 wasn't sure but that she had black hair. And nobody who looked at Florence

Burns, who sat complacently fanning herself, could have the slightest doubt that she was the blondest of the blonde and always had been. It was the day of establishing for history the fact that a George Washington, under proper treatment by the minions of the law, might become an Ananias. The hearing did not end then, but the methods of the investigators seemed to have impressed themselves on Justice Mayer's mind. The prosecution put Mrs Brooks on the stand and she swore that the comb found in Room 12 belonged to Florence Burns. Mr Brooks told of the girl's threats. But nobody found the pistol, and no waiter came to say that Walter Brooks dined that night with Florence Burns – or anybody else.

On 22 March, five weeks after the murder, the hearing came to an end.

'This has been an extraordinary case in more than one respect,' said Justice Mayer. 'It is evident that if the case were decided on the evidence furnished by the prosecution without any corroboration – as would have been the case before the grand jury – an indictment probably would have been returned. The threats this defendant is alleged to have uttered against the life of Brooks would be important if it were proven that this defendant was with Walter Brooks in the Glen Island Hotel on the night in question. It seems strange that, after the girl made these threats, she was permitted to remain under the same roof as Brooks.

'But the entire case turns on the question, was the defendant in the hotel with Brooks on 14 February, and was the side-comb found in that room after the crime her property?'

'That this girl could have been mistaken by the bellboy for a dark-complexioned girl is beyond the realms of possibility. From this and other facts I have enumerated, I find that there is not enough evidence to connect the defendant with the crime charged. I find that Walter Brooks was murdered in the Glen Island Hotel on the night of 14 February, but there is no evidence to connect Florence Burns with the murder. The defendant is discharged.'

Then Mr Backus whispered to Florence, and the girl stopped fanning herself and smiled up at the man on the bench who had set her free.

It is anti-climatic not to end Florence Burns's story there, as a love story should end, but ugly stories come to ugly ends.

Florence Burns married late that year, after she had made an unsuccessful attempt to be an actress. Her husband was Charles W. Wildrick. In 1908 she sued him for divorce. Two years after that, she and a man named Edward H. Brooks were found guilty of extorting money from Charles Hurlburt, a Brooklyn man, by means of the badger game.[1] She and Brooks had been living together. In October 1910, she and Brooks were sentenced to serve not less than seven years and five months in Sing Sing.

Florence Burns, when the prison van took her away to prepare for her trip up the river, looked little like the very pretty girl who was charged with killing Walter Brooks. Her face had been lined by alcohol, her clothes were shabby, and her hair, still golden, looked as if she had lost a comb – another comb.

[1]EDITOR'S NOTE: *Dictionary of American Underworld Lingo* (Constable, London, 1950): 'Victims are enticed into compromising positions. The blackmailer then appears on the scene, claiming that the girl is his wife or sister. Extortion follows.'

# *A Particular Bed of Dahlias*
## H.B. Irving

In the year 1882, Mademoiselle Elodie Ménétret, a lady forty-two years old, living in Paris, had the misfortune to lose her pet dog, Rigolo. Whilst still in the first agony of her affliction, Mlle Ménétret happened to go into a shop in the Boulevard Haussmann, to buy a pair of boots. As she was making her purchase, she saw a lady pass by leading a dog, which she thought she recognised as the lost Rigolo. Before she had time to confirm her belief, the lady had disappeared. In her anxiety to recover her pet, Mlle Ménétret asked the woman who kept the shop whether she might return there for a few days to watch, in the hope that the lady with the dog that so closely resembled her Rigolo might pass by again. The woman of the shop, her name was Euphrasie Mercier, gave a ready consent. Mlle Ménétret fully availed herself of the permission accorded her, and, as a result, the two women became friends.

They were not long in finding out that they both came from the same part of France, the department of the Nord, which lies in the extreme north-east of the country, touching the Belgian frontier. Euphrasie Mercier had a long and distressing story to tell of repeated misfortune, of afflicted and dependent relatives, of the approaching collapse of the boot business; in the latter event, she said, she should try to find a place as a lady companion. Mlle Ménétret, who was lonely and something of a 'malade imaginaire', had recently bought a little house at Villemomble, in the neighbourhood of Paris. Euphrasie

142

Mercier seemed kindly, religious, and unfortunate. When Mlle Ménétret took up her residence at Villemomble in the March of 1883, she engaged Euphrasie Mercier as her companion and housekeeper. Thus it was that out of the small beginning of the lost Rigolo, there sprang up an intimacy which cost Elodie Ménétret her life.

This life had been peaceable enough, if not strictly speaking respectable: one of those lives which, over-shadowed at the beginning by some inglorious accident, seem unable to throw off the evil spell attaching to their unhappy birthright. The father of Elodie Ménétret had been killed in Africa in the course of some exploit of illicit love; his dishonourable death had slowly killed his wife, and left their children orphans. Elodie had been well educated, but her history, as one writer happily phrases it, had been the common history 'of those young ladies who drift from music lessons into dalliance'. Before she reached the age of forty-two, she had entertained a certain number of lovers, and they had been comparatively generous lovers. Besides a permanent allowance made her by one of them, she had amassed a small fortune of some £3,500. Such was the present state of the lady who had accepted the kind offices of Euphrasie Mercier.

Euphrasie Mercier was sixty when she met Mlle Ménétret. She also was one of an ill-fated house. Her father, who had given up teaching for spinning, had left a fortune of more than £16,000, but it was a fortune doomed to be of little profit to his descendants. Of his five children, three were mad. Religious mania was the form of insanity that possessed the Mercier family. The high-sounding names he gave to his children show something of the kind latent in the father; he called them Euphrasie, Zacharie, Camille, Honorine, and Sidonie. Of these, the last three were unquestionably the victims of pronounced religious mania, believing themselves guilty of imaginary sins, and writing extravagant letters to the Pope and their Bishop, in which they claimed to be in direct personal communication with God; the son Camille was firmly convinced that in the course of one night a steam-engine had absorbed his brain. Euphrasie and her brother Zacharie had alone escaped the family curse. Though the former was certainly eccentric, it was an eccentricity that stopped well short of insanity; what was religious mania in her brother and sisters became in her something like sinister hypocrisy; there was method in her occasional exaltation and her furious appeals to divine co-operation; if she called God as a witness or summoned him as her avenger, it was either to back a lie or to gratify some settled hate. Euphrasie was cunning, resolute, and courageous, and devoted to her crazy relations whom, she declared, heaven had committed to her charge. But she was never successful in business. By the year 1848 her management of the paternal inheritance had resulted in its complete dissipation.

Then began her wanderings, which extended as far as Vienna, in search of a livelihood for herself and the three daft ones, Camille, Honorine, and Sidonie. For some thirty years this singular quartette led a precarious and nomadic existence, pursuing their erratic course over parts of Central Europe and much of the South of France. In 1878 they found settlement in the home of a Polish countess, who seems to have been over-inclined to charitable offices. But even her goodwill was not proof against the arrogance and excitability of Euphrasie, and the idle vagaries of her half-witted brood. She was obliged to dismiss them from her house. It was then that Euphrasie started the boot shop in Paris, whilst her brother and sisters were eking out a miserable existence in a neighbouring district.

In 1882, when she first made the acquaintance of Elodie Ménétret, Euphrasie Mercier was sixty years of age. For nearly forty years she and her odd companions had tramped life; after four years of unsuccessful business, the boot shop was on the verge of bankruptcy – repeated failure seemed to promise no term to their fruitless wanderings. How if the adventure of the lost dog should prove the threshold of a haven of rest? Villemomble the last stage in their frantic progress?

Within a month from her arrival at Villemomble, Mlle Ménétret began to find her elderly companion rather alarming. She had been for some time a sufferer from nerves. In the boot shop Euphrasie Mercier had been sympathetic enough with her condition, but in the new home the old lady, with her pale, wrinkled face and hooked nose, seemed to take a strange delight in exciting rather than allaying her mistress's affliction. She began to trouble and distress her with horrid stories of ghosts; she told how solitary women had been strangled in their beds by cruel murderers, to rob them of their gold. The poor woman became so apprehensive of some sinister design on the part of her weird companion that she summoned a neighbour, Mlle Grière. 'The boot maker frightens me,' she said to her, 'I have dismissed her, but she obstinately refuses to go, saying she only wants food and lodging.'

The two women, in their agitation, drew up a list of Mlle Ménétret's jewellery and other valuables, of which Mlle Grière made a copy. This was on 18 April 1883. Elodie Ménétret was never seen again.

'Mlle Ménétret is dead to the world,' said Euphrasie Mercier to all enquirers: 'she has entered a convent, and I have sworn not to divulge the place of her retreat.' The house at Villemomble was rigidly closed to every comer. In vain did the sister of Mlle Ménétret communicate her not unreasonable suspicion of some foul play to the Commissary of Police at Montreuil. Though that functionary went so far as to summon Euphrasie Mercier to appear before him, he was quite satisfied when the old lady produced a letter, which she said she had just received from Elodie, bearing the somewhat inconclusive date of 'Wednesday evening'. Euphrasie Mercier at the same time produced a document which she was pleased to style a 'deed of gift'. It said, 'I quit France – I leave all to Mlle Mercier – let her transact my affairs.' True, this document was somewhat formless, written in a hand that betrayed agony of body or agitation of mind, in fact a document full of unpleasant suggestion, but it was unquestionably in the handwriting of Mlle Ménétret, and that was sufficient for all practical purposes. Closer investigation seemed unnecessary, nay superfluous, to the Commissary of Police at Montreuil.

In the meantime, the conduct of Euphrasie Mercier was marked by an assurance which could only have arisen from very definite information on her part as to the whereabouts, and present circumstances and intentions, of her vanished friend. Less than a week after Mlle Ménétret was said to have quitted Villemomble for ever, the idiot brood was installed there, and decked out with the clothes of the departed lady; other portions of her clothing were sold to a Jewish dealer. At first Euphrasie Mercier was reluctant to conclude the bargain with the Hebrew woman, owing to her strong anti-Semitic prejudices; and it was only when the latter promised to convert her daughter and marry her to an uncircumcised husband that the zealous old lady finally agreed to the sale. In August of the same year, Euphrasie Mercier made a journey to Luxembourg. There she visited a notary to whom she described herself as one Elodie Ménétret, a lady who had come to reside in Luxembourg. Having property at Villemomble, in France, she wished to draw up a power of attorney in favour of a friend, Mlle Euphrasie Mercier, who was to administer her French property. The notary making some little difficulty as to her identity, Euphrasie Mercier stepped out into the street and soon returned with two witnesses – a musician and a hairdresser – who, at a modest cost of five francs a head, were only too pleased to declare that this lady was indeed well known to them as Mademoiselle Elodie Ménétret. Fortified with her fraudulent power of attorney, Euphrasie Mercier returned to Villemomble, and did not hesitate to remind two gentlemen who made small allowances to Mlle Ménétret that their quarterly payments were overdue.

There was a particular bed of dahlias in the garden at Villemomble which Euphrasie Mercier strictly forbade the gardener to touch. Dogs were rigidly excluded from the garden, Mlle Mercier having a not unnatural prejudice against their too frequent habit of scratching up the flower beds.

For two years Euphrasie and her three demented relatives were the sole occupants of the house at Villemomble, but in 1885 their number was increased to six by the arrival of two visitors. One was Adèle Mercier, daughter of Euphrasie's brother Zacharie, the other a certain Chateauneuf, an illegitimate son of the mad sister, Honorine, by a Comte de Chateauneuf. The latter was a red-headed and altogether unpromising youth, physically and morally unprepossessing; he had been living at Brussels, a deserter from the French army, and he was disguised as a woman when his Aunt Euphrasie smuggled him to Villemomble. She regarded Chateauneuf with that intense and uncompromising affection which she lavished on all her immediate relatives. But, in this instance, that affection was to compass her utter ruin. In her blind devotion she failed to see that the youth was treacherous and hypocritical to the last degree. Though shortly after his arrival he ran away with his cousin Adèle, and married her at Brussels without his aunt's permission, Euphrasie readily forgave him, and welcomed the young couple back to Villemomble.

Chateauneuf was curious as well as treacherous, and he was not long in detecting that there was some mystery that oppressed and troubled the weak-headed denizens of his aunt's strictly secluded home. His gibbering aunts, Honorine and Sidonie, kept letting fall odd sayings about the dead coming to life, and misfortune coming out of the garden; the power of attorney obtained by Euphrasie at Luxembourg seemed to him suspicious; the close watch set over one particular bed of dahlias, an extravagant precaution. He began to indulge in that dangerous intellectual operation known as putting two and two together, in spite of the obvious inconvenience that he saw it caused his loving aunt, Euphrasie. The more the estimable young man pondered, the more clearly it appeared to him that, if Elodie Ménétret had disappeared she had disappeared within the four walls of his aunt's abode, and that the old lady knew something in regard to the vanished woman which she was particularly anxious to conceal.

Euphrasie Mercier's own indiscretion finally resolved her nephew's doubts. Honorine, during the war of 1870, had embroidered a banner in honour of the Virgin Mary. This was now set up in the house at Villemomble, and candles were kept constantly burning before it. Euphrasie would on occasions prostrate herself in front of this banner. She would then kiss the ground sixteen times, crawling backwards all the while, after which, rising to her feet, she would throw open the window and cry out, 'In the name of God, get hence, Beelzebub, Lucifer, and thou, Satan! Hence with your legions of devils! Back, judges, commissaries, Assize Court! Back, ye terrors that beset me! Back, phantoms of my garden! Family of Ménétret, rest in peace – in the peace of God, and the glory of the elect! Amen!'

This singular ceremonial was not lost upon the assiduous Chateauneuf; it confirmed his blackest suspicions, at the same time constituting a base of operations from which to levy tribute on his affectionate aunt. But in her case avarice triumphed over affection. When Chateauneuf pressed Euphrasie for money, and threatened denunciation if his suit were rejected, he was met with an unflinching refusal. Thereupon the indignant virtue of the young man, hitherto not ineffectually stifled or concealed, broke into feverish activity. He withdrew to Brussels, whence he addressed two letters, one to the judicial authorities at Paris, the other to an uncle of Elodie Ménétret. The first was a dutiful, though reluctant information against his good aunt; in the second he declared with a fitting show of horror, that Elodie Ménétret had been poisoned with chemical matches, her body burnt and buried in the garden, and that he had thoughtfully inscribed on the wall of the room in which she had been murdered, 'Mademoiselle Ménétret killed here!'

In consequence of these communications Euphrasie Mercier was arrested and a judicial investigation opened. In a spot in the garden pointed out by Chateauneuf, the bed of dahlias so carefully preserved by Euphrasie Mercier from the attentions of man or beast, was found a quantity of charred bones, and some teeth, one of which had been stopped with gold. The medical experts declared the bones to be those of a woman of forty-five, the approximate age of Elodie Ménétret; and that lady's dentist, by referring to his books, proved that he had stopped one of her teeth with gold. An examination of the bulbs of the lilies and dahlias which were buried with the bones enabled an expert to fix the date of their disturbance as the spring of 1883, the time of the disappearance of Mlle Ménétret. In her bedroom some greasy stains were found in front of the fireplace; and the soot in the chimney was declared, after analysis, to contain matter similar to that found in the chimneys of restaurants where they are in the habit of cooking a quantity of meat. A knife and a chopper were discovered in the house; but there was nothing in their appearance to suggest that they had been used for an improper purpose.

But there was one discovery made, which was significant under the circumstances, if not very cogent as a piece of evidence. This was a cutting from the *Figaro* newspaper of 18 October 1881, giving the details of the murder of a priest at Imola in Italy. It had been stuffed behind a looking-glass. The following was the paragraph to which the attention of the magistrates was directed:

What has become of the victim? The search for him has at last been successful. Yesterday the body of the priest was discovered in a pit of moderate depth that had been dug under the country house of Faella (the suspected murderer). It was buried at a depth of about eighteen feet and covered over with a quantity of rice.

This story may have suggested to Euphrasie Mercier the method by which she was alleged to have concealed the remains of Elodie Ménétret.

If the direct evidence of the murder of Mlle Ménétret by her companion and housekeeper was of a rather slight description, a very strong circumstantial presumption was raised in favour of her guilt. Enquiries were made in all directions to find out the convent in which, according to the prisoner, Elodie Ménétret was immured. But they were fruitless. On the other hand, the proceedings of the prisoner, subsequent to the alleged departure of her mistress, were one and all those of a guilty person, desirous of hiding and profiting by some crime, and the discovery of the charred bones of a woman of Mlle Ménétret's age, coupled with the evidence of the nephew Chateauneuf, seemed to point very clearly to the nature of the crime which the old woman was so anxious to forget by prayer and invocation.

How, in what fashion, Mlle Ménétret, if murdered, had met her death was a secret known only to the prisoner; these two were alone in the house at the time. Whether she was poisoned as Chateauneuf declared, or put to death in a more summary fashion, there was no conclusive evidence to show. If the bones in the garden were hers, her body must have been disposed of by dismemberment and burning in a stove. There can be little doubt from the various hints and suggestions which the mad sisters were in the habit of dropping to different people, that they were aware that the house at Villemomble was haunted by the presence of some crime with which their resolute sister was directly connected. Not only did they first arouse the inquisitive suspicions of Chateauneuf by their vague allusions to the mystery of the garden, but to an architect, who had come to the house at the request of Euphrasie Mercier to design some improvements, Honorine Mercier made a very damning statement. The architect, worried by the importunities of the mad sisters, who followed him about singing chants and invocations, in a moment of irritation asked Euphrasie why she did not get the Commissary of Police to take these women away. 'Oh,' said Honorine, 'the Commissary indeed! If once he came here, Euphrasie would never see the light of heaven again!'

But, in spite of their evident knowledge of something sinister with regard to their elder sister, Honorine, Sidonie, and Camille were found to be too insane to be of any service to justice, and shortly after their arrest, they were all three shut up in the lunatic asylum of Sainte-Anne. Euphrasie alone was summoned to the Bar to answer for the murder of Elodie Ménétret. She, according to three eminent authorities on brain disease, was fully responsible for her acts; she was, they declared, certainly affected by the religious mysticism prevailing in the family, but in a very much less degree than her sisters, and not in a degree which interfered in any way with her capacity for rational crime.

On 6 April 1886, the trial of Euphrasie Mercier commenced before the Cour d'Assises for the Seine department, sitting in Paris. M. Dubard presided. On the table reserved for the 'pièces à conviction' was a large jar containing the charred remains dug up from the dahlia-bed, and declared by the prosecution to be those of Elodie Ménétret.

Euphrasie Mercier met the searching questions of the President with fanatical resolution. True to the family tradition, God was her ever-present stay and comfort, dictating all her actions, and ready to put her enemies to shame and confusion. By His orders she had purchased property; she declared that it was she, and not Elodie Ménétret, who had bought the house at Villemomble, and that she had purchased it with her own money and at God's direction, in order that it might serve her as a retreat before making a pilgrimage to Mount Nebo. 'But,' urged the President, 'it was Mlle Ménétret who paid for it.' 'With 15,000 francs that I had lent her,' retorted the prisoner.

'Have you the receipt?'

'No, I don't understand business.'

'As a matter of fact, you were her servant?'

'We had agreed to let it appear so. I wanted to keep my pecuniary circumstances a secret from my family, whom I had been keeping all my life. I was getting old, and I wanted to reserve a part of my savings for God.'

'You took up your residence at Villemomble on 30 March 1883?'

'Yes, on a Saturday. Mlle Ménétret wished to go in on a Sunday, but I told her that that was unlucky.'

The President pointed out to her that she had certainly produced a receipt, signed by Mlle Ménétret, for 15,000 francs, and dated 1878; but that unfortunately the watermark of the paper on which the receipt had been drawn up was dated four years later, 1882. The prisoner had presumably made use of a blank signature left behind by the dead woman. The President went on to recall to her mind the fearful stories by which she had so worked on the fears of her mistress, and named an old gentleman to whom Elodie Ménétret had confided her state of terror. 'An old thing of seventy-five!' exclaimed the prisoner, 'who wanted to gobble her up and who said he was livelier than a young man of twenty-five!' In reply to the President, she gave her version of Mlle Ménétret's disappearance, 'She had made up her mind to flee the world. She was in love with a young man whom she could not marry. She worshipped him as the angels worship. Besides, she was afraid to live in the house; sinister individuals had been seen skulking about the premises. One evening she threw herself at the feet of a priest, and the next day, after spending the night in burning all her letters, she departed.'

'That is your version. You are aware, however, of what the prosecution allege? They say that Elodie Ménétret never quitted the house at Villemomble, that she was buried there, and that you murdered her.'

'Impossible! I, who wouldn't hurt a cat or a rabbit! I, to kill a poor lady I loved so dearly!'

'Where is she?' asked the President.

'I don't know.'

'You have given many and various accounts of her where-abouts. You have said she was in Paris, another time in Belgium, then in Luxembourg, and Mecklenburg.'

'She often changed her convent. I have seen her in the dresses of different sisterhoods. She used to write to me.'

'Where are her letters?'

'I sent them all back to her by her own orders. She was dead to the world, and was afraid lest any indiscretion should divulge her place of retreat.'

'The police have made active enquiries in all the convents in France and the neighbouring countries, but in vain.'

'So I am told.'

'Have you seen her?'

'Often!'

'Where?'

'At night. Once, for instance, under the clock of the Gare du Nord.'

'Do you know of any convent where they would tolerate such escapades?'

After questioning the prisoner as to a letter, purporting to come from Elodie Ménétret, but in reality a forgery by the prisoner, and taking her through the journey to Luxembourg to obtain the fraudulent power of attorney, the President arrived at the point in the story when the ill-omened Chateauneuf appeared on the scene. In 1885, after two years' residence at Villemomble, Euphrasie Mercier had lapsed into her usual state of pecuniary embarrassment, and had sent for her niece Adèle Mercier from the North of France, that she might make the house over to her by a fictitious transfer, and so avoid her liabilities. But the prisoner now explained that the real object of this transfer was to facilitate the marriage of her niece with her cousin, Chateauneuf.

'You were very fond of your nephew, Chateauneuf?'

'Yes, unluckily for me. All the same, the spirits had warned me that this child would be my ruin.'

'He was a deserter. You brought him from Brussels to Villemomble disguised as a woman?'

'Not I, but his cousin, Adèle. On her return I noticed that she seemed very tired. But I very soon understood her fatigue, when I saw that she and Chateauneuf occupied the same room at Villemomble.'

'What happened then? Was it that you talked too much? Did you betray yourself to, or confide in Chateauneuf? In any case he discovered your secret.'

'What secret?'

'The death of Mlle Ménétret.'

'Mlle Ménétret is not dead.'

153

'Chateauneuf acquired the firm belief that you had murdered her.'

'He is conspiring with my enemies.'

'No, not that. He asked you for money, and, when you refused him, he denounced you to the judicial authorities.'

'Oh yes, yes, he wanted to go to America, and asked me to help him to get there. I said to him, "My child, I have no ready money, but when I have. . . . " He would not wait. Satan had possessed him with a devil of greed.'

'It is significant that accompanying his letter to the Procureur was a plan of the garden at Villemomble, and particularly of the flower bed beneath which he said the remains of Mlle Ménétret would be found. And, as a matter of fact, they were found there.'

'What were found? Enough bones to fill a pocket-handkerchief! The garden is an old cemetery.'

'It is nothing of the kind. No other skeleton has been found there except that one, which is lying on the table there among the "pièces à conviction".'

After the President had enumerated the various circumstances already given, which made in favour of the prisoner's guilt, the interrogation concluded:

'When, the day after the disappearance of Mlle Ménétret, your sister Honorine arrived at Villemomble, you seemed to be worried. "I have just carried through a great work," you said, "the angels have helped me."'

'I had tidied the garden and cleaned the walls. God has always given me strength when I have stood in need of it. For the last three days I have been in a dying state, unable to eat anything, yet today I have been able to speak to you for four hours on end, with nothing but a couple of eggs in my stomach. I am innocent. Act as your conscience shall direct you.'

'Your case has enjoyed an extraordinary publicity. If Mlle Ménétret is still living, she, whose virtue and piety you laud to the skies, she, whom you saw daily and with whom you have corresponded incessantly, she, your friend and confidante, would come to your deliverance, or at least would communicate with your judges, if she were so anxious to remain in absolute seclusion. Look at that skeleton (*pointing to the bones on the table*) and swear that those are not the poor remains of Elodie Ménétret.'

'Before God, I swear it! I have never killed a soul, and when my time comes to appear before my Sovereign Judge, I shall go straight to heaven!'

The culminating interest of the trial was in the evidence of the prisoner's two relatives, her nephew Chateauneuf, and his wife and cousin, Adèle.

'I am the daughter of Zacharie Mercier,' said the latter. 'My father lives in the department of the Nord. My Aunt Euphrasie persuaded me to come to Villemomble. She showed me the papers of Mlle Ménétret, said that she was her heiress, and that there was no fear of the lady ever returning to claim her sous. At Villemomble I was told that Euphrasie had found a treasure. My aunt showed me her will, which, she said, was made in my favour, on condition that I protected all the mad members of the family. "When I die," she added, "you are to bury me in the garden – one may just as well sleep in the earth as in a coffin."'

'Did not your Aunt Euphrasie tell you that a very long time ago the garden at Villemomble had been a cemetery?'

'No. It was my Aunt Honorine who said to me one day, "There are corpses in the garden. We must go and find the priest to bless them." Chateauneuf also knew a great deal. One day in my presence, he looked hard at my Aunt Euphrasie, and said, "Terrible things will come to pass here. The dead will speak."'

'You are mad, Adèle! How can you say such things before these gentlemen?' said the prisoner, beside herself.

'Did your aunt ever show you some hair that had belonged to Mlle Ménétret?'

'Yes, sir, a long plait of blonde hair,' exclaimed the prisoner.

'It was a false plait! Wretched child, how can you say such things? I, who have been so good to you! You have deceived me! The Holy Virgin will punish you!'

155

The witness was removed amidst the continued threats and curses of her frantic aunt.

Chateauneuf appeared on the third day of the trial. His truculent compound of vanity, cant, and malice created anything but a favourable impression, though his evil character made his extraordinary evidence the more probable. 'I ought to warn you, gentlemen,' said the President, addressing the jury, 'that this man is an informer.' 'Yes,' echoed his aunt, 'and he is my nephew, the man who used to write to me as his beloved aunt.'

Without looking at the prisoner, Chateauneuf began, 'I am twenty-seven. I was brought up by my father. As a child I was quite able to reckon up my Aunt Euphrasie. She used to make me go on my knees, and then tell me I should see the Virgin Mary; but, as I was very naughty, I didn't see the Virgin, and got smacked instead. My mother, Honorine, was as mystical as my aunt. In 1878 I joined the army, where I greatly distinguished myself (*he was a deserter*). I then went to the United States. There I received letters from my Aunt Euphrasie. She told me that she had become rich, and made me promise to come back to her.'

'That is true. By God's permission, I had recovered the money I had lost,' said Euphrasie.

'My aunt smuggled me into France. 'You must come back,' she said, "or I shall die!"'

'You lie! You are a deep scoundrel. God will punish you.'

'Come to the facts,' said the President. 'Soon after you entered the house at Villemomble, you guessed that Mlle Ménétret had been murdered?'

'I did. I wrote on the wall of her dressing-room, "Mademoiselle Ménétret killed here."'

'How was it that you found out this secret?'

'The power of attorney my aunt showed me struck me as suspicious. I asked her what had become of Mlle Ménétret, and she could not tell me. Besides, I saw her constantly looking in the direction of the dahlia-bed. My religious scruples (*cries of 'Oh! Oh!' from his listeners*) obliged me to try to discover how she had come into possession of her fortune.'

'Then you discovered this crime by a process of deduction?'

'Oh! I could play the spiritualistic game as well as they; I said that I had seen visions as well as they, and that the day would come when the dead would speak. I wanted to give them to understand that I had guessed at the murder.'

'Go on, talk on! Tell all your lies! You're wasting your time and these gentlemen's too. You have taken me in completely, I thought a man who had once been a Capuchin was sure to be honest,' exclaimed Euphrasie, enraged.

'At length I was able to point out the exact spot where the bones would be found.'

'Bones buried by my enemies in the garden at Villemomble. God had forewarned me of it.'

'Why did you inform against your aunt?' asked the President.

'For the salvation of her soul. I did not want her to burn for ever in hell-fire. I did not want the gates of paradise to be closed to her because of an ill-gotten fortune (*loud burst of laughter*). Besides, I was acting in the interests of society. My aunt was intending to murder somebody else in similar circumstances, at least so I believed . . . In conclusion I left Villemomble and wrote to M. Kuehn, the head of the Detective Department.'

Euphrasie: 'Wretch, you are my murderer! M. Kuehn died all of a sudden, because he sought to do me ill.'

This disinterested protector of society and his aunt's ultimate salvation hurried from the witness box that he might not tarry in France until his free conduct had expired, when he would have been immediately arrested as a deserter. But before he left, the prisoner's counsel reminded the unselfish youth that he had been trying to sell in the purlieus of the court a penny leaflet entitled *The Mystery of Villemomble*, by Alphonse Chateauneuf. His wife was unable to escape without a final malediction from her energetic aunt. She had been recalled on some point in her evidence. As she was about to leave the box, Euphrasie thus addressed her: 'You should not tell lies. I do not wish it, and I forbid it. You little hussy! The Devil possesses you! God commanded me to fast three days and three nights in order to drive the devil out of your body, you little Judas!' The only person to whom the prisoner addressed any words of kindness or approval was the Commissary of Police at Montreuil, who had so readily accepted her dubious explanation of the sudden disappearance of Mlle Ménétret. He was hailed as a 'good Commissary', and rewarded by a kindly glance from the old lady's eyes.

In the course of the four days' trial, those facts with which the reader is already familiar were fully substantiated by evidence which the prisoner, for all her appeals to heaven and hell, was powerless to shake.

On 10 April, after an hour and a half of deliberation, the jury found Euphrasie Mercier guilty of murder, theft, and forgery, but granted her extenuating circumstances. She was sentenced to the utmost punishment to which this verdict and her age could by law expose her, that of twenty years' imprisonment. In France, penal servitude was not inflicted on those over sixty years of age. The prisoner received her sentence in silence; the hopelessness of the situation made prayers and curses superfluous.

Euphrasie Mercier, though beyond doubt sane, was surely eccentric. It is the atmosphere of eccentricity surrounding her horrid deeds that recalls irresistibly to the mind the weird creations of Poe or Lefanu; whilst the boding chorus of her demented relatives is strongly suggestive of those strange and fateful beings that inhabit the palaces and parlours of the Maeterlinckian drama.

# A Root of Some Evil

From the Stockport Advertiser (Cheshire), 11 December
1863

Alice Hewitt, alias Holt, was indicted for the wilful
murder of Mary Bailey, her mother, at Stockport,
on 27 March last. The prisoner was a widow, and
for some time before her mother's death had been
cohabiting with a man named Holt, passing as his wife.
The deceased was also a widow, and resided with Holt
and her daughter at 43 Great Egerton Street, Heaton
Norris, in the borough of Stockport. The prisoner was
in poor circumstances, and she and Holt evidently
regarded her mother as an encumbrance.

There appears to be considerable competition between the life insurance offices at Stockport. Of
these there is one called the Wesleyan and General
Assurance Society, which insures for very small sums,
and receives the premiums in weekly and fortnightly
payments; 6d a week, it seems, would insure £28 on
death. The prisoner had been canvassed for this society
in January last, and on 18 February, her mother falling
unwell from bronchitis, she agreed to insure. The
mother did not recover sufficiently to go before the
doctor, so the prisoner applied to a lodger, Ann Bailey,
to go with her and pass the doctor as her mother. Ann
Bailey refused, and she then said she would send for
Betty Wood, as Garlick, the canvasser for the society,
had told her anyone would do to pass the doctor. She
did not send for Wood, but got one Elizabeth Wells
to go with her to Peter Scarlett, the agent of the

society, and represented Wells to be her mother. The examination was passed, and the necessary certificate was obtained from the medical man.

The deceased was attended by the union surgeon, and up to 1 March was improving. The insurance was effected on 6 March. On the 12th the infirmary surgeon visited the deceased and found her suffering from sickness. She said she had great pain in her stomach. Ann Bailey was about this time sent on several occasions for some pies, which were always warmed by the prisoner, and it was observed that they caused vomiting in all who partook of them. The infirmary surgeon varied his remedies, but without arresting the symptoms, and he observed that the medicine was not regularly given to the deceased. The union surgeon was also attending the deceased, but neither of the surgeons knew that the other was visiting her.

The woman died on 27 March, early in the morning. The symptoms were consistent with arsenical poisoning, and not with bronchitis. A few days before the old woman died, one Catherine Ryan was in the house, and saw the prisoner throw some of the medicine into the fire. Ryan said, 'I'd never go for medicine and throw it away.' The prisoner said, 'H – to them and their medicine.' She went up to bed, and in coming down again said, 'Is my mother dead?' Ryan said, 'No, nor signs of it. It is to be hoped she'll recover.' The prisoner said, 'Tut, tut, Mrs Ryan.'

The daughter also, it seems, bought some arsenic at the shop of Mr Davenport, a druggist. On one occasion, having bought some arsenic, she said to Ann Bailey, 'Ann, you mustn't say anything at all about this here.' Bailey said, 'About what?' She said, 'About this arsenic,' and Bailey said, 'No.' That evening, about nine o'clock, the prisoner asked her mother if she would have some brandy and water, and she said 'Yes'. The prisoner then went out with a cup, and after an absence of half an hour returned with some brandy in the cup, but would not let her mother drink

160

of it for some time, as she said she had grated a root into it and wanted it to dissolve. When the mother took the brandy, her daughter seemed vexed that she had not drunk up the dregs, and this cup was afterwards found strongly impregnated with arsenic.

When the old woman died, the prisoner went into Ann Bailey's room, and said, 'Well, Ann, I am very glad my mother's dead. I've all my clothes fast [pawned], and I wanted this money to release them. If she had not died it would have been God help us.' She also said, 'If she had not got the money, her husband [Holt] would have beaten her.'

On 8 April Scarlett paid the prisoner £25 16s, the amount of the insurance money. The deceased was disinterred on 12 June, in consequence of the discovery of the fraud that had been practised on the insurance company and of various rumours that were in circulation, and it was found fully impregnated with arsenic. One hundred and thirty grains were found in the body, twenty-six times as much as would destroy life. . . .

The jury, after an absence of twenty minutes, found the prisoner GUILTY, with a recommendation to mercy. On hearing the verdict the prisoner fainted, and moaned in a way pitiful to hear.

His Lordship assumed the black cap, and, after a few appropriate remarks suitable to so solemn an occasion, and promising to forward the recommendation of the jury to the proper quarter, although he could hold out no hope that the prayer would be complied with, he proceeded to sentence the prisoner to DEATH.

The wretched woman was then removed from the dock in an insensible condition.

While the court was dispersing, the 'public' mani-fested considerable feeling against the witness Holt. They cried, 'Fetch him out,' and looked as though they were prepared to offer violence to him on his appearance outside; but, by the advice of some person connected with the prosecution, who noticed this hostile expression, he jumped into the dock and made his way through the jail. Thence, by changing his hat to disguise himself, he managed to escape to the railway station.

The jury's recommendation having fallen on deaf influential ears, Alice Holt was executed, at Chester, on the Monday after the Christmas weekend of 1863. The event attracted an audience of only a few thousand (in-prison hanging was still five years away), but the printer and the audience-infiltrating pedlars of copies of the following ballad had done nicely from advance sales.

> *A dreadful case of murder,*
> *Such as we seldom hear,*
> *Committed was at Stockport,*
> *In the county of Cheshire;*
> *Where a mother named Mary Bailey*
> *They did so cruelly slaughter,*
> *By poison administered all in her beer*
> *By her own daughter.*
>
> *The daughter insured the life of the mother*
> *For twenty-six pounds at her death,*
> *Then she and the man that she lived with*
> *Determined to take away her breath.*
> *And when Betty Wood represented the mother,[1]*
> *She didn't act with propriety,*
> *For the poor mother lost her life,*
> *And they swindled the Society.*
> *Now that old gal's life's insured,*
> *Holt to the daughter did say,*
> *Better in the grave she were immured,*
> *And the money will make us gay.*
> *[Alice said:] Now that you have got me in the family*
> *    way,*
> *And from me my virtue you've wrung,*

[1]EDITOR'S NOTE: William J. Skillern, Head of Reference Services, Stockport, suggests that 'if Elizabeth Well's name be written as "Betty Wells", it not very different from "Betty Wood", and it is possible that the writer of the verses was confused over the two names'.

You'll never be happy, not a day,
Till on the gallows I'm hung.

She laid a plan to murder her,
As we now see so clear,
To put a quantity of arsenic
Into her poor mother's beer.
To see her lay in agony
Upon that dreadful night,
With a dreadful dose of arsenic,
Oh, it was a dreadful sight.

She lived but just six hours,
Then the poor woman did die,
And this base murdering wretch
The dreadful deed did deny.
On the man Holt she laid the blame,
Vowed he did her mother slay,
Holt on her did just the same,
Saying she took the mother's life away.

But there's no doubt the base wretch
Did her poor mother slay,
For which on Chester's scaffold
Her life did forfeit pay:
So all young women a warning take
By this poor wretch you see,
A hanging for the mother's sake
On Chester's fatal tree.

# The Murderer Was a Lady
*Miriam Allen de Ford*

There can be no doubt that Louise Peete was thoroughly guilty of both the murders for which she was convicted, and for the second of which she was gassed at San Quentin in April 1947 – the second woman in the history of the State of California to incur the supreme penalty. Indirectly, she also caused the death of at least one other person, and perhaps of three beside him.

Louise Peete (she always preferred the name conferred on her by her longest marriage) was born in Shreveport, Louisiana – just when is a matter of conjecture. She was an incorrigible liar, and in nothing more than in her age. The best that can be said is that she arrived on earth somewhere between 1880 and 1892. The median date, about 1885, makes her sixty-two or thereabouts on the spring day when she departed from this planet. Her maiden name is lost in the mist that surrounds her – she didn't keep it long – but her given name seems originally to have been Lofie Louise. She soon dropped grotesque 'Lofie' and remained simply Louise thereafter.

Her father, she said (there was no other evidence), was a schoolteacher. 'I have never considered myself particularly well educated,' she averred modestly. Somehow she developed a rather good epistolary and oratorical style, she did quite a lot of solid reading, she was an accomplished needlewoman, and knew something about practical nursing, and she was musically gifted, with a voice that deserved and had had some training. 'I covet only two things,' she told an interviewer in 1927,

'– spiritual understanding and culture.' And she was decidedly personable, even in middle age. She was short, inclined to plumpness, but pleasingly so, with chestnut hair and grey eyes, which though described by one ungallant reporter as 'porcine', really were one of her best features. 'She was the clubwoman type,' remarked Clinton Duffy, then warden of San Quentin. 'If you had met her without knowing who she was, you would have thought her a leader of civic activities in some suburban town.' She used her looks, but it was not beauty of which she was vain – though she did, in one of her rare lapses from equanimity, quarrel violently with a cellmate in the Los Angeles County Jail over which of them had the prettier feet.

According to her own version, she led in youth 'a sheltered life that did not permit of drinking and smoking, consequently I have never adopted either habit'. According to Alan Hynd, who delved more realistically into her history, she was a young hellion, in Shreveport and later in Boston. This interlude in the Hub, according to her was to study for the opera, though Boston is seldom selected for that purpose; according to Hynd, it was a predatory foray among the Brahmins which ended in presentation of a sizable bribe by her victims to persuade her to get out and stay out. It was preceded by her first marriage, in 1903, to Henry Bosley. They were soon divorced, and some accounts say that Bosley committed suicide in 1906. If not, then he was the only one of her husbands who did not kill himself.

In any event, from Boston Louise went to Dallas, where in 1913 she met Harry Faurote, a hotel clerk. Hynd says she married him. There is no proof of that, but it is indubitably true that Faurote was found dead with a bullet in his head, and that a diamond ring was missing and Louise was questioned by the police. The ring was found later, and she was released without charges.

She turned up next in Denver, where in 1915 she married Richard Peete, a salesman. Peete is one of the most pathetic figures in the whole story. He was a quiet, humdrum, home-loving man, thoroughly respectable, unambitious, and not very strong. He was devoted to his wife and to the daughter, Betty, who was born a year after their marriage, and he stood by firmly through the terrible shock which came to him in 1920. It is true that he divorced her after her first conviction, but she insisted that she had asked him to do so for the child's sake, and even after the divorce he wrote to her in prison wishing he could 'exchange places' with her. In 1924, in Tucson, Arizona, he committed suicide. The little girl was reared by relatives in the East and probably changed her name.

It is possible that the child was the one person for whom Louise Peete ever really cared. Her husband came to Los Angeles and stayed with her throughout the Jacob Denton trial, and the four-year-old baby was in the courtroom too. After Mrs Peete went to San Quentin, Betty was told that her mother was in a hospital. Louise seldom wept, but she shed tears then. 'I love that little child with all my heart,' she said. 'The one shining light in my present plight is that my daughter has such a father as Peete.'

But her family ties had not prevented Mrs Peete from leaving Denver for Los Angeles early in 1920. Later she said that she and her husband had had a 'slight quarrel', then that he was ill and she had to make money to care for him, finally that he was planning a business trip to the Orient, and she went to the coast to await his return. In this case, it seems strange she did not bring the baby with her. 'How different things would have been if I had gone with him to the Orient as he wished!' she sighed. He did not go to the Orient.

The first fatal moment in Louise Peete's life was drawing near. She answered an advertisement and under-took to lease a house on South Catalina Street, not far from Rosedale Cemetery, belonging to a wealthy middle-aged widower named Jacob C. Denton. She was never Denton's house-keeper, as the papers called her later. Whether (as Hynd alleges) she was something more – Denton continued to live in the house – is of interest only to the neighbourhood gossips. What is certain is that after 30 May Denton disappeared, while Mrs Peete stayed on in the house. In fact, she held parties in it, she sold various valuables from it, she ordered clothing on Denton's charge accounts, she forged his name on cheques, and on at least one occasion she signed her name on an official paper as 'Mrs J. C. Denton'. She sublet the house twice – neither deal was concluded – and she took in a rowdy set of boarders. In the midst of this, Denton's nephew and his daughter by his first marriage began to make enquiries.

Louise Peete was one of the most superbly imaginative liars on record. She never made up a small story when a big one would do. To all enquiries she had an answer. Denton, it appeared, was in hiding; he was humiliated because he had lost an arm. It seemed that he had had a visitor, a 'Spanish-looking woman', with whom he had quarrelled violently, and who had knifed him – causing his arm, apparently, to drop off. That was why she had signed his name on cheques – or, alternatively, she had met him at his hiding place, and he had laid his hand on hers while she signed, thus making it 'legal'. There were other versions of the story, some related at the trial or after the conviction. They contradicted one another and they were all wildly improbable, but she told them all with the utmost blandness.

Another little difficulty in the ex-Denton ménage came out later. That was the question of the load of earth – or was it fertiliser? – dumped in the cellar, which Mrs Peete was going to use in the garden; and the trouble with the furnace, which, when it was used, 'made a noise like a graveyard groan'. To repair this, she called in an unusual character who described himself as a 'heater expert, actor, vocal teacher, and licensed real estate dealer' – he was also an ex-burglar. He testified that Mrs Peete had asked him urgently if it would be necessary to enter 'the crypt'. The crypt, she said, she had had built in the cellar to preserve some of Mr Denton's belongings to which he was especially attached. She had indeed.

After Denton's body had been discovered in the cellar in September, and an X-ray examination had showed he had died of a bullet wound in the back of his neck, Mrs Peete, who had returned to Denver, was asked to come to Los Angeles to shed light on the mystery. She came voluntarily with her husband, but her stories failed to impress the police. In January 1921 she was put on trial for the murder of Jacob Denton.

About the only defence that could be made, in the face of the overwhelming evidence, was that she would not have been strong enough to bury Denton's body, and would have been afraid to live on in the same house with it. It was not good enough. She was sentenced to life imprisonment.

In San Quentin's women's department, Louise Peete reigned as a sort of queen. The only serious contender for the throne was Clara Phillips, who had battered her rival to death with a hammer; and Mrs Phillips lacked the grand manner. In 1927 Mrs Peete gave a newspaper interview from which one unfamiliar with her situation would scarcely have guessed it.

'The public must be educated to our needs,' she said. 'We need stepping-stones and people send us roller-skates. We don't ask for the advantages of a country club or a university, but we seek curative treatment so that when we are liberated we shall be prepared against any recurrence of the so-called mental illness that brought us here.

'There should be some way, too, of segregating the better educated, more refined women from those who have been brought up in close touch with life's slime and filth. They should be protected against being sullied by it.'

She turned wistful. 'I wish I could see a sunrise or a sunset. It has been so many years since I have watched the glories of either. When I am freed some day, I shall seek a high hill near the Pacific and lose myself in the sunset. Then I shall wait for the dawn, to see the new day come again in the East.'

As San Quentin is magnificently situated on San Francisco Bay, and there are plenty of windows, it is difficult to see why Mrs Peete had been barred from viewing either sunsets or dawns. Perhaps she could not enjoy them except in the open air.

In November 1933 all the women in San Quentin were transferred to the new California Institution for Women at Tehachapi. Mrs Peete went with the rest. The next time she saw San Quentin, more than thirteen years had passed, and she was about to be executed for another murder.

In April 1939 she was paroled, on her tenth application. A shrewd observer remarked that she would 'make headlines again one of these days; she is too used to being a personage'. She was allowed to take a pseudonym – Anna B. Lee. She spent her first days of freedom in a guest-cottage, making curtains for a rest-home for girls. Later, during the Second World War, she operated a canteen for servicemen in Los Angeles. A woman tenant in the building suddenly 'dropped from sight', leaving her home in disorder. Some enquiries were made, and the *soi-disant* Mrs Lee explained that the woman had injured her hip and died of the injury. For some reason there was no further investigation. In 1943 her parole-officer, Mrs Latham, with whom she had been living, died (of natural causes), and Mrs Peete was transferred to the care of her old and good friend, Mrs Arthur Logan, in Pacific Palisades. Before she left Mrs Latham's home, she thriftily took with her an object that the dead parole-officer would not be needing – a .32 Smith & Wesson revolver.

Arthur and Margaret Logan had become interested in Louise Peete when she was at Tehachapi, had visited her often there, and had become her warm friends. They were delighted to have her come to live with them. By this time Mr Logan was an old man, slipping into senility. There was nothing wrong with him but loss of memory and extreme vagueness of mind, but there is no doubt that he got on Mrs Peete's sensitive nerves. For the present, however, she had more important things to think about – namely, getting her hands on some of Mrs Logan's money and property. The Logans were not really wealthy, as Denton had been, but they were very comfortably off.

The whole tangled financial plot began again. There was a story of a trust fund due Louise in Denver, with

which she would pay her half of a joint lease with Mrs
Logan on the Pacific Palisades house; tickets were bought
for both of them to go to Denver, but were never used.
There were misunderstandings and explanations that did
not explain, and an atmosphere of dissatisfaction about
which Mrs Logan could do very little, and Mrs Peete very
much. The chief problem was Mr Logan, who, however
deteriorated mentally, could hardly fail to notice it if his
wife disappeared. At Mrs Peete's suggestion, he had been
sent to the Los Angeles General Hospital for psychiatric
observation, but they sent him home again after nineteen
days.

There was another complication. In May 1944 Mrs
Peete had married again. Her new husband was an elderly
widower from Glendale, a bank messenger named Lee
Judson. He knew her as Anna Lee and had not the
remotest idea of her previous history. She did not inform
the Logans of the marriage. Judson continued to live in a
hotel in Glendale, and his wife merely visited him there.

Suddenly all this was changed. The last time anyone
saw Margaret Logan alive was on 30 May, twenty-four
years to the day since Jacob Denton had disappeared.
She too, it seemed, had gone on a trip. Her husband
grew annoyingly persistent about her, and when he was
told she was ill in a hospital, he could not understand
why he could not visit her. In June Mrs Peete finally
succeeded in having him committed to the State Hospital
for the Insane in Patton. He died there in December, still
wondering in his lucid intervals why his wife of so many
years had turned against him and never came near him.
It was perhaps the second cruellest thing Louise Peete
ever did: the implication of Judson in her crime was the
cruellest. She did not even pay for Logan's funeral, but
had his body handed over to the medical college at Loma
Linda.

Now began the cheques signed in Mrs Logan's name,
the objects sold, the house taken over. Judson, to his
bewilderment, had been told in June that his new home
was to be in Pacific Palisades. Mrs Logan, his bride's
'foster sister', had gone away, and Mr Logan would soon

170

follow her. Judson moved in, no glimmer of suspicion in his trusting soul.

Unfortunately, the State of California was not so credulous as Lee Judson. Mrs Peete had been paroled to Mrs Logan, and the monthly reports had to be sent in. They continued to arrive promptly. They were glowing – too glowing. The Parole Board grew leery. Even so, it was not until December – two weeks after Logan's death in Patton – that they investigated.

There was no 'crypt' this time; Margaret Logan was buried under an avocado tree in her own garden. Louise was a creature of habit; Mrs Logan, too, had been shot in the back of the neck, as she sat at the telephone – perhaps, as has been surmised, to report to the authorities some of the things she had found out about her protegée's frauds and pilferings. But she did not die immediately; she had to be finished off with the butt of the pistol.

It would not have been Louise Peete if she had not had a beautiful story prepared. Yes, she acknowledged, she had buried Mrs Logan's body – under her favourite tree. But she had not killed her. Mr Logan, deceased, had done that. He had suddenly gone violently insane and had beaten his wife to death. Mrs Peete had realised that this put her in an awkward position, in view of her past; so she had thought it best to dispose of the corpse and keep the whole affair to herself.

Poor Judson, shocked and flabbergasted, was taken along as accessory.

On 12 January 1945 he was exonerated. On 13 January he jumped out of a thirteenth-storey window of an office building.

'Our life together was so beautiful,' said his widow. 'He told me, "If you ever leave me I'll take sleeping-powders."'

Then she pulled herself together. She spent the trial reading *The Importance of Living*, by Lin Yutang.

There were eleven women and one man on the jury. They were not out very long. On just about the anniversary of Denton's and Mrs Logan's deaths, Louise Peete was sentenced to die. The State Supreme Court refused a writ of *habeas corpus*, and the United States Supreme Court twice refused to review the case. Twice her execution was postponed on the grounds that new evidence was forthcoming; it did not appear. Two years after her conviction, she was brought from Tehachapi to San Quentin for execution. She was very tired when she arrived, but she had only one complaint to make to Warden Duffy. The officers who drove her had sounded the siren all the way; it was conspicuous and embarrassing, and no way to treat 'the dowager of Tehachapi Prison'.

Until the last minute, she could not believe that the sentence was to be carried out. 'Governor Warren [Earl Warren, who later became Chief Justice of the Supreme Court] is a gentleman,' she said, 'and no gentleman would send a lady to her death.' But the governor, with notable lack of courtliness, said that there were no extenuating circumstances, and refused to save her from the gas chamber.

Her self-possession never failed her. Attired in a grey and burgundy print street-dress, her still unturned hair simply arranged, she walked from the condemned cell across the hall to the death-chamber with a firm, brisk step. She sat down in the green metal chair without being ordered to do so, and looked on with interest as the straps were adjusted. She smiled graciously at Warden Duffy, and her lips formed the words, 'Thank you'. Then she closed her eyes and waited for the gas to work.

Louise Peete seems truly to have been one of those of whom William Bolitho said that their self-compassion 'sucks the meaning out of every existence but their own,' whose lives are 'a serial adventure in which each episode is complete in itself, whose master-plot is known only to themselves'.

Indubitably she was able to persuade herself, for the moment at least, of the truth of every one of her falsehoods. Listen to her as she waited for her trial for the murder of Denton:

'I am able to preserve an attitude of calm because I am innocent. I have no visions of a murdered man to shake my

172

nerves; no torments of remorse to disturb my sleep. There are other women in this jail who are charged with the murder of men. Some cannot sleep. Perhaps their minds mirror death agonies. I have seen them pace the floor and wring their hands. I have felt tremendous sympathy for them. My heart has been wrung with the wish that I could help them. At the same time I have thanked God that I am not tormented as they are.'

Can anyone doubt that the very sound of these words transformed Louise Peete – while she spoke – into the noble, wronged, innocent creature she described herself as being?

Her calm and self-possession were sublime. They were almost stolid. All through the accounts of her trials, such phrases occur as 'perfect poise', 'bright and fresh', 'as calm as ever', 'she did not lose her composure'. 'There will be no screaming or hysterics,' she assured reporters. 'I am not built that way.' Yet there is plenty of evidence that beneath the calm was a quick and irritable temper; she was easily angered, but nearly always she could control her anger and bide her time. Only once, during the Logan trial, when Captain Thad Brown, chief of the homicide squad, testified to a conversation with her, she screamed, 'Why don't you tell the truth?' Asked if she was nervous, she answered, 'No, but I am humiliated.'

Somehow it seems to have been impossible for her to think that the world could fail to take her at her own estimate. She justified to herself everything she did; so why wouldn't other people take her word for it? When she was informed of Peete's suicide, she said, 'His health was poor and I think he felt remorse of conscience. If I could have confided in him I wouldn't have got into the trouble I did.' Richard Peete, to her mind, killed himself because he had failed his wife, not because she had ruined his life.

She spoke always with the utmost tenderness of her own child. 'I feel the same things that other mothers feel. I want her to have the best environment, the best teaching, the best of everything. I have tried to get her these things, to shield her from the things that were not the best.'

173

Yet this is the same woman who included among the things she stole from Jacob Denton a pathetic pair of baby shoes and a baby book marked 'In memory of Dolly and Baby – keepsakes' (Dolly was his second wife, who had died in childbirth.)

The one obsession she never lost, the one pose that was no pose because it was genuine delusion, was that of her perfect gentility and delicacy. She might, on occasion, scream and fight like a virago; she might suddenly descend into underworld argot, or dance with mad joy over full ownership of her victim's possessions; probably she had had, as Hynd contends, her years of promiscuity, near-prostitution, blackmail, and even drug-addiction; she had certainly murdered two human beings and disposed of their remains without a quiver: but with it all, to Louise Peete, Louise Peete was a great lady. The theme recurs constantly in her conversation. 'I am not embittered, only saddened at times.' 'I have read how, when fish swim beyond their depth, they are crushed by the force of the water. I don't want that to happen to me. I won't let it.' 'My sense of honour and sentiment kept me quiet [about Denton's mishap at the hands of the mythical "Spanish-looking woman"].' 'I am innocent – it would be silly to lie.' 'I am ready to accept the inevitable. I have made my peace with God and the world.'

In her very last interview, almost her last words on earth, she sounded the same note so often heard before:

'I come from cultured, educated people, and I have a background of culture. My parents were not delinquents, and they did not rear delinquent children.'

She probably inhaled her first whiff of cyanide-acid gas, fully convinced that she was a gentlewoman whose life had been full of misfortune and misunderstanding, but who to the end had upheld the banner of refinement.

# And to Hell with Burgundy
### Dorothy Dunbar

Some women attract men; some women attract trouble. Florence Bravo was a double-barrelled magnet; she attracted both. Her small voluptuous figure, which no corset or bustle could distort, her coquettish chestnut hair, which no curling iron or crimpers could restrain, and an irresistible siren song of helplessness made up a small but potent package of sex appeal. It was just her luck to fatally fascinate an alcoholic, a married man and a spoiled boy.

As for trouble, Florence was a feather, caught in every emotional downdraught that came along, and she got trapped in some cross-ventilation when she overstepped the unalterable code of Victorian womanhood. In an age when the sanctity of woman was as jealously institutionalised as chivalry had been in the days when knighthood was in flower, the pattern of Victorian dualism fell into inflexible categories. A woman was either 'pure' or 'fallen'. She had to be one or the other, and there was no room for a twilight zone, such as our current popular myth of the 'prostitute with the heart of gold'. A pure woman was a virgin with chaste thoughts and sexual *rigor mortis*, a woman who granted her husband bleak conjugal submission and periodic heirs, or a spinster who lightened the heavy load of her days with the subliminal sop of John Ruskin's Italian-art criticism or pure-thinking literature like *Sesame and Lilies*.

A fallen woman encompassed everything from the dashing, feather-boa-ed belles, who toyed with champagne and men in private dining-rooms, to gin-logged slatterns. But Florence Bravo didn't realise that never the twain shall meet. If she had followed the rigidly mapped course of either a good or bad woman, there would have been no nineteenth-century shocker known as the 'Balham Mystery', but because she wanted to have her cake and eat it, too – Florence Bravo was just plain murder.

Florence Campbell was the daughter of Robert Campbell, a wealthy London merchant. Everything points to a spoiled, petted childhood and to a familiar twentieth-century spectacle – well-meaning parents who are unable to cope with the teenage Frankensteins they have created.

In 1863, when she was eighteen, Florence visited Montreal, and, to her, one of the greatest attractions of the brave new world was Captain Ricardo of Her Majesty's Army. Captain Ricardo listed as assets a dashing uniform reminiscent of a Strauss operetta, a name with an evocative Latin ending, and a comfortable fortune. In 1864, two doom-ridden events took place: Maximilian, that harassed Hapsburg, became Emperor of Mexico; and Florence Campbell married her colourful captain. Some men accept marriage with stoicism, while others luxuriate in the matrimonial state. There are men who fight it – wifebeaters, etc., and there are men who avoid it, e.g. bachelors. Captain Ricardo, by nature and inclination, belonged to the latter group. He had an inordinate liking for women, and he was an avid companion of the grape. Florence, at a dewy, well-developed eighteen, certainly must have appealed to him, but marriage was the price for capitulation. So Captain Ricardo bartered bachelorhood for maidenhood.

Like most young brides, Florence embarked upon matrimony with high hopes. Perhaps she even subscribed to the age-old delusion that marriage changes a man. In any event, the honeymoon came to an abrupt end when it became apparent that 'hearth and home' were just two rather unfamiliar words in the English language to Captain Ricardo. He was keeping mistresses and making a cult out of the empty bottle. To Florence, spoiled and petted, six years of violent scenes, pitying smiles from friends and relations, and a husband's total lack of concern over her happiness were devastating blows to her ego. Captain Ricardo alternated between sessions with pink elephants and fits of black remorse, and in the middle of this emotional maelstrom was Florence, her self-confidence shaken, her ego badly fractured. To help soften the ugly edges, she herself started drinking. If you can't beat 'em, join 'em, seemed to be her attitude. Let there be no mistake that Florence's drinking fell under the proscribed limits of social drinking for Victorian females. The sip of sherry or blackberry wine, the gulp of stronger spirits for medicinal reasons, were not for Florence. She drank as she did everything else – wholeheartedly, on the spur of the moment, and all the way. Any self-respecting AA would unabashedly tip his hat to the capacity of this frail Victorian belle.

By 1870, Florence was on the verge of what would now be called a nervous breakdown. Six years of marriage to Captain Ricardo plus the solace of the vine was just about all an emotionally weak woman could stand. Mr and Mrs Campbell suggested that Florence and her captain go to Malvern, a famous spa in Worcestershire, to take the cure, but it was useless. Captain Ricardo had retired from the army and was now devoting his full time and energy to drinking, so Florence's parents insisted upon a deed of separation. In the following April, Captain Ricardo died in Cologne as he had lived – with a transient mistress in his bed and the eternal bottle at his elbow. His will was unaltered, and Florence was now set to become a very merry widow with an income of £4,000 a year to be merry on and Dr Gully to be merry with.

In 1842, Dr James Manby Gully had developed a water cure and offered it to an ailing public. Dr Gully was no quack. He was a thoroughly trained medical man, and his water cure put the town of Malvern on the map, so to speak. Applications of water were used in every form – packing in wet sheets, compresses, spinal washes, friction with dripping towels – and his patients included

Tennyson, Carlyle, Charles Reade, Bulwer-Lytton, an all-star cast from the social register, and many other water-sodden Victorian greats and near greats. Dr Gully himself had literary aspirations. He wrote articles on medical subjects and wrote a play adapted from Dumas's *Mademoiselle de Belle-Isle*, which was produced at Drury Lane in 1839. Dr Gully was sixty-two at the time Florence came to Malvern with her problem-husband. He is described as handsome, if not tall, with clean-cut features and an erect bearing. He wa also the possessor of disastrous amount of personal magnetism, and a wife in her eighties whom his water-cure could not help; she had been in an insane asylum for thirty years.

It was this man that Florence met when she came to Malvern. At the time she was emotionally ill, and Dr Gully's warmth and sympathetic understanding must have been every bit as effective as his water treatments. Florence was head-strong but not self-reliant, and Captain Ricardo had proved a broken reed upon which to lean. Dr Gully, a pillar of strength by comparison, was a welcome change from Captain Ricardo's highhanded, drunken treatment and grovelling sober remorse. Florence recovered under his care. Today, when everyone nonchalantly tosses off the argot of psychoanalysis, transference is an everyday word, and Gully's age was no detriment after Florence's experience with a young husband. Picture Dr Gully, well-to-do, attractive, respected, confronted with a rampant Florence seething with devotion and flattery.

Just when Dr Gully's bedside manner began to assume personal overtones is not clear. Florence steadfastly maintained that nothing improper had occurred during her marriage to Captain Ricardo. However, early during her widowhood her parents refused to see her because of her relations with Dr Gully and because of her continued drinking. For four years, Florence was cut off from her family and was beyond the possibility of a social circle, but she had Dr Gully, emotional security, and her wine.

It was during this isolated, if not celibate, widowhood that Mrs Cox entered the scene. Florence was visiting her solicitor, Mr Brooks, and there she met Mrs Jane Cannon Cox. Mrs Cox was the down-at-the-heel widow of a Jamaican engineer with three sons, and through the kind offices and advice of a Mr Joseph Bravo, who had interests in Jamaica, she had bought a small house in Lancaster Road, Notting Hill, London, as an investment, had placed her sons in a school for destitute gentlefolk, and obtained the post of governess to Mr Brooks's children. Mrs Cox, with her solid figure inclined to dumpiness, heavy-featured face, glittering spectacles, and skintight hairdo was no beauty, but she made up for it by relentless efficiency, an air of unassailable respectability, and a grim desire to please.

It wasn't long before the pretty but lonesome widow appropriated Mrs Cox as her companion. And it was, at the time, an ideal arrangement for sheltered, beautiful Florence and plain, unsheltered Mrs Cox. Mrs Cox ran Florence's house, controlled the servants, and understood perfectly the comfort and elegance that Florence wished to enjoy, without exerting any effort. And Mrs Cox had it made. She had exchanged the life of uncertainty, drudgery, and poor pay of a governess for the role of 'friend of the bosom' to Florence Ricardo. They were on the footing of social equals; it was 'Florence' and 'Janie'. She received a salary of £100 a year, clothes, and incidental expenses, and her three boys could spend all their school holidays with her.

In 1872, Dr Gully sold his practice amid testimonials and demonstrations from the citizens of Malvern, and, wherever Mrs Ricardo lived, Dr Gully's home was sure to be within spitting distance, and their friendship continued. In 1873, the pair made a trip to Kissingen, and the tangible result was a miscarriage. During this illness, Mrs Cox attended Florence, but claimed she did not know the real nature of the trouble.

In 1874, Mrs Ricardo moved into what was to be her permanent home, the Priory. It was a pale-tinted structure with arched windows and doorways, winding walks, flower beds, melon pits, a greenhouse, and the house was luxurious with a sparkling Venetian glass collection, a lush conservatory with ferns that cost 20 guineas each, and every expensive horror of Victorian decoration. Here Florence Ricardo settled down, with the perpetual Mrs Cox, to enjoy life's three greatest pleasures – gardening, horses and drinking. And Dr Gully, whom one is tempted to nickname Johnny-on-the-spot, bought a house just a few minutes from the Priory. There were lunches, dinners, drives, and several nights of illicit bliss when Mrs Cox was away. Dr Gully had a key to the Priory. Then, one day in 1875, Mrs Cox wished to call on her benefactor, Mrs Joseph Bravo, and Mrs Ricardo went with her. There she met Charles Bravo, the spoiled son of the house. The meeting itself was without incident, but its repercussions are now called the Balham Mystery.

In October 1875 Mrs Ricardo and Mrs Cox went to Brighton and there again met Charles Bravo, a sulky handsome young man with a weak chin. He was a young man her own age of her social position, and when Florence returned to the Priory she told Dr Gully that she was going to break off their 'friendship' and reconcile with her family because of her mother's health. Actually, Florence was, in all probability, weary of her 'back street' existence. She had snapped her garter at the world, and, instead of being told she was cute, was knuckle-rapped by social ostracism. What she did not tell Dr Gully was that she was also going to marry Charles Bravo. Dr Gully was hurt when he found out about the engagement, but later wished Florence happiness. Perhaps the demands of a young capricious mistress had begun to tell on the sixty-seven-year-old doctor, and the prospect of placid days and monastic nights had an attraction.

But in spite of Florence's injunction that they must never see each other again, they did. According to British law at that time, every possession and all property of a woman marrying automatically became the property of her husband, unless specifically secured to her by settlement. Florence wanted the Priory and its furnishings secured to her, but Charles sulked and muttered that he wanted to sit in his own chairs or he'd call the marriage off. Florence arranged a meeting with Dr Gully to discuss the impasse, and they met at one of the Priory lodges. Dr Gully advised her to give in on the matter and wished her luck. As usual, Florence backed down, and 'Charlie' won the moral victory of 'sitting in his own chairs'.

Charles Bravo was not a wealthy man in his own right and was mostly dependent on his father's spasmodic handouts, since his law practice only netted him £200 in the last year of his life. However, his future was bright. He was his step-father's heir, and his prospects for becoming a Member of Parliament were good, and here was a young, infatuated, wealthy widow, with a belated yearning for respectability and security, palpitating on his doorstep.

Charles and Florence told each other 'all'. He had had a purple passage with a young and willing woman in Maidenhead but had made a final settlement with her before breaking off. Florence told him about her idyll with the autumnal Dr Gully, and Charles seemed to accept it with equanimity. Charles was what might be called 'rotten spoiled'. He was charming when things went his way; extremely conscious of money, probably because he had been around it so much, yet had so little of his own. And the prospect of marrying a wealthy widow – even one with a sexual slip-up in her past – was attractive. Certainly he was not consumed with jealousy. When he went to see Florence's attorney about the settlement, he received the lawyer's congratulations with the remark, 'To hell with the congratulations, it's the money I'm interested in!'

Mr Bravo, Sr, settled £20,000 on Charles as a wedding present, but Mrs Bravo refused to attend the wedding. She didn't like Florence. For that matter, she probably wouldn't have liked any girl her son married. And so Florence and Charles Bravo were married and settled down at the Priory, and they might have lived happily ever after if Charles Bravo hadn't been so stingy.

They seemed like an average, happy couple. Charles brought his business associates to dinner and heartily endorsed the institution of marriage. The servants all thought the Bravos a happy, devoted couple, but Mrs Cox was worried. Charles was cutting down on the overheads. He wanted Florence to give up her horses and her personal maid, and he wanted her to dispense with Mrs Cox. He had put together a pound here and a pound there and figured out that the genteel companionship of the widow was costing £400 a year – enough to keep a pair of horses. And Florence, who operated on an anything-for-the-sake-of-peace basis and who was charmed by her young attractive husband, decided to give up her horses and maid, and Mrs Cox could see the handwriting on the wall. Her relatives in Jamaica had been pressing her to return, and now Mr Joseph Bravo and his son were urging the same thing.

During this period of surface serenity, some curious events occurred. Mrs Cox had several meetings with Dr Gully; whether they were planned or accidental, they have all the aspects of Mrs Cox trying to stir something up. Mrs Bravo had had a miscarriage, and Mrs Cox, at one encounter, asked Dr Gully, who knew Florence couldn't take regular opiates, to send something to her house in Lancaster Road. The doctor sent some laurel water and thus laid himself open to later insinuations that he was supplying Mrs Bravo with abortive medicines – a rather empty charge in view of the fact that a child would have been just what Florence Bravo needed to cement her newly established respectability and reconcile Charles's mother to the marriage. And then, just after Charles Bravo figured out the cost of Mrs Cox's companionship, he was taken suddenly and mysteriously ill one morning on his way to his chambers in Essex Court. So ill, in fact, that he reported to his father that he was afraid people might think he was drunk from the night before – a nonsensical thought for he had the digestion of an ox.

That was the situation at the Priory at Easter weekend, 1876. Charles Bravo had his attractive wife and her equally attractive fortune. Florence was recovering from her miscarriage and appeared devoted to her husband,

and Mrs Cox was brooding about the imminence of a trip to Jamaica. Charles Bravo laid out a tennis court, played with Mrs Cox's boys, who were down for the Easter vacation, and wrote to his mother that he had 'loafed vigorously and thoroughly enjoyed the weekend'.

On Tuesday, 18 April, Mrs Cox set out to look at houses in Worthing (where the Bravos were planning to go for Florence to recuperate from her miscarriage) and with her she took a flask of sherry to fortify herself. Mr and Mrs Bravo drove into town, and he went to his club for lunch, while Florence, after doing some shopping, returned to the Priory for lunch, which she polished off with a bottle of champagne. Mrs Bravo understandably spent the afternoon resting. Late in the afternoon, Mr Bravo returned home and went horseback riding. The horse threw him, and he returned home with his dignity and himself rather badly bruised. Mrs Bravo suggested a warm bath before dinner, and then went upstairs herself to change. Mrs Cox returned from her house-hunting with a photograph of the house, and, it is presumed, an empty sherry flask. She did not have time to change for dinner; she did go upstairs to clean up a bit.

Dinner, consisting of whiting, roast lamb, a dish of eggs, and anchovies on toast, was not a sparkling meal. Mr Bravo was still smarting, both literally and figuratively, from his fall. Mrs Bravo had dry pipes from the champagne and was trying to put out the fire with sherry, and Mrs Cox had things to think about. Mr Bravo drank his three customary glasses of burgundy, but the ladies put him to shame. Between them, Mrs Bravo and Mrs Cox polished off two bottles of sherry, and the butler later testified that he had decanted the usual amount of wine that evening.

After dinner, they retired to the morning room, where again conversations languished. In about half an hour, Florence announced that she was going to bed and asked Mrs Cox to bring her a glass of wine. Since her miscarriage Mrs Cox had been sleeping with her, and Mr Bravo had been relegated to a guestroom. Mrs Bravo went upstairs and was followed by the obliging Mrs Cox with a glass of wine. Mary Anne Keeber, a maid, came in to help Mrs Bravo undress and was asked by Mrs Bravo to bring her some wine. Mary Anne brought a tumbler of marsala and was still in Mrs Bravo's room when Mr Bravo entered to make the understatement of the Balham Mystery. He accused his wife of drinking too much wine and stormed off to bed. Mary Anne withdrew, noting as she left the room that three-bottle Florence had taken the count and was asleep, while Mrs Cox sat by her bed fully dressed. As Mary Anne started downstairs, the door to Mr Bravo's room flew open and he cried, 'Florence, Florence. Water!'

And Mrs Cox, who sat fully dressed and wide awake by Mrs Bravo's bedside, heard nothing until Mary Anne called her. From the time of Mr Bravo's cries for water, there began a procession of doctors and a progression of statements by Mrs Cox. Mary Anne and Mrs Cox rushed into Mr Bravo's bedroom, where they found him standing by the window vomiting. Mrs Cox ordered Mary Anne to rush for an emetic and Dr Harrison. When Dr Harrison arrived, Mrs Cox told him that Mr Bravo had taken chloroform to ease a toothache, but the doctor said there was no smell of chloroform.

Mrs Bravo was by this time aroused, and sent for Dr Moore and Royes Bell, a Harley Street surgeon and friend of the Bravo family. Mrs Bravo threw herself down by her husband, spoke to him fondly, and promptly fell asleep and finally had to be carried to her own room. Obviously, she hadn't had time to sleep it off.

Dr George Johnson arrived with Royes Bell, and they were told by Mr Bravo that he had rubbed his gums with laudanum for his toothache.

'But laudanum,' Dr Johnson told him, 'will not account for your symptoms.' Mr Bravo stubbornly insisted that he had taken nothing else, no other drug.

At this point, Mrs Cox took Mr Bell aside and confided to him that, while 'Charlie' was vomiting at the window, he had told her, 'I have taken poison. Don't tell Florence.'

Mr Bravo's reply to this was, 'I don't remember having

spoken of taking poison,' and he again insisted that he had only rubbed his gums with laudanum. Dr Harrison was annoyed with Mrs Cox for not telling him about the poison. 'You told me,' he said petulantly, 'that he had taken chloroform.'

Mr Bravo by now was in a bad way. He was frequently sick and had intense stomach pains, but he kept his wife by him, drew up a will leaving everything to her, and sent word to his mother to 'be kind to Florence'. Again he swore to the growing assembly of doctors that he had taken nothing but laudanum and, with a trace of his old money-consciousness, said, 'Why the devil should I send for you, if I knew what was the matter with me?'

Mr and Mrs Joseph Bravo arrived, and the elder Mrs Bravo took charge of the sick room. However, when the doctors had declared the case hopeless, Florence roused herself from her despair and her hangover to take action. 'They have had their way, and I as his wife will have mine.' And proceeded to try water treatments and small doses of arsenicum, both considered by the doctors to be harmless.

Then Florence called in Sir William Gull, a physician who wore as a crown the credit for having cured the Prince of Wales of typhoid fever.

'This is not a disease,' Sir William told Bravo. 'You have been poisoned. Pray tell me how you came by it.'

But Bravo persisted that he had taken nothing but laudanum. On Friday morning, 21 April, the much harassed, much questioned man mercifully died.

The inquest had more of the air of a family tea than anything else. Mr Carter, the coroner for East Surrey, was informed in a note written for Mrs Bravo by Mrs Cox that 'refreshments will be prepared for the jury', and the inquest was held in the dining-room of the Priory. Mr Carter, an experienced official, had the idea that there was something amiss, and, out of deference to two respectable families, did not even send notices of the inquest to the papers. Test of specimens and organs revealed that Mr Bravo had died from a large, economy-sized dose of antimony administered in the form of tartar emetic, which is easily soluble in water and tasteless. Mr Joseph Bravo went to Scotland Yard, and Inspector Clark, an expert on poisoning cases, was instructed to make enquiries to see if antimony could be traced to the Priory. Both Mrs Bravo and Mrs Cox had medicine chests, and the house contained innumerable bottles of medicine, but there was nothing lethal. Still, Mr Joseph Bravo refused to believe Mrs Cox's story that his son had committed suicide.

The coroner felt it was an embarrassing case of suicide, however, and closed the hearing without allowing Drs Johnson or Moore to testify and without calling Mrs Bravo, who was suffering from shock. The verdict was 'that the deceased died from the effects of the poison antimony, but there was no evidence as to the circumstances in which it had come into his body'.

Mr Bravo was buried on 29 April, and Mrs Bravo and Mrs Cox, probably fortified by several flasks of sherry, departed for Brighton. But the end was not in sight. Charles Bravo had been popular in his circle of acquaintances and colleagues, and they were dissatisfied with the summary verdict from the coroner's inquest. A week later, *The World* ran a provocative paragraph titled 'A Tragedy?' It was done in the gossip-column style of today, with no names mentioned: Charles Bravo was referred to as 'a rising young barrister recently married'.

The following day, 11 May, the *Daily Telegraph* became more explicit, naming names and premiering the sobriquet, 'The Balham Mystery'. The *Telegraph* also commented on the secret and unsatisfactory inquest and called for a re-opening of the investigation. The case aroused great interest, and journals and newspapers were deluged with suggestions as to how Mr Bravo had clashed head on with the antimony. Two schools of thought emerged. The fatal dose had been administered either in his burgundy at dinner or in the water jug, which sat on his night-stand and from which he was in the habit of drinking before he went to bed. Because of the time element, the water jug was a 2-to-1 favourite. The doctors in the case were bitten by the literary bug.

Drs Moore and Harrison wrote for the *Daily Telegraph*, and Dr Johnson gave a medical history in the *Lancet*.

Mrs Bravo was aware of the drift of public sentiment; she was receiving anonymous letters. On the advice of her father, she offered a reward of £500 to anyone who could prove the sale of antimony or tartar emetic 'in such a manner as would throw a satisfactory light on the mode by which Mr Bravo came to his death'.

The Home Secretary (afterwards Lord Cross) issued a statement that his office was 'entirely dissatisfied with the way the enquiry had been conducted'. Mrs Bravo's consent was obtained for a thorough search of the Priory. The investigation lasted two days; every medicine in the house was tested. Nothing was discovered that Charles Bravo could could have taken, but five weeks between Bravo's death and the investigation were ample time to get anything incriminating out of the way.

On 27 May a private enquiry was called, and, although Mrs Bravo and Mrs Cox were not asked to give evidence, they both asked to make statements. Mrs Cox's statement, made after consultation with Mr Brooks, her former employer and Mrs Bravo's solicitor, dropped a bombshell. She deposed that, through a misguided effort to shield Mrs Bravo's character, she had not given full particulars at the inquest. What Mr Bravo had actually said was, 'I have taken poison for Gully – don't tell Florence.' However, Mrs Cox had to admit that Mrs Bravo had had no contact with Dr Gully since her marriage, and characterised her relationship with Dr Gully as 'very imprudent' but of an innocent character. Mr Bravo had a hasty and violent temper and four days before his death had had a violent quarrel with his wife in which he called her a selfish pig, wished he were dead, and said, 'let her go back to Gully.' He constantly said that he hated Gully.

Mrs Bravo's statement said that Bravo had pressed her constantly to cut down on expenses and turn away Mrs Cox. That he was short-tempered and had once struck her, that his mother was always interfering, and that he read all her mail. She had told him about her attachment

187

to Gully, and he had told her of his kept woman at Maidenhead. Florence, in this statement, described her relationship with Gully as innocent. 'Nothing improper had ever passed between us.' Mrs Bravo said that her husband had constantly harped on Gully after their marriage. The day he had taken ill, they had had a fight about Gully on the way to town. Florence refused to make up. 'You will see what I do when I get home.' He thought she drank too much sherry, but she had given it up to please him. (Certainly one glaring untruth in Mrs Bravo's statement.)

On the strength of this private enquiry, Mr Clark was ordered to hold a new enquiry with a fresh jury. It opened on 11 July 1876, in the billiard room of the Bedford Hotel next to Balham Station. If the first enquiry had been a furtive affair, the second was a field-day for the public. The room was crowded with newspaper reporters and the curious, of which there were many. After the jury had viewed the exhumed body through a small piece of glass in the coffin, a grim legal formality, Mr Joseph Bravo testified that Charles had been full of life, that he was interested in forensic medicine, and that they were on intimate terms. He had never heard Charles mention Gully's name. The last three letters Charles had written to his family, just before his illness, indicate that he was in the best of spirits.

Mr Joseph Bravo said that Charles had discussed Mrs Cox with him, saying that he had nothing against her, but that she cost too much. He himself had agreed and had advised Mrs Cox to return to Jamaica. She had said she would not return. Mr Joseph Bravo also commented that while Charles was dying, Mrs Bravo did not 'appear much grieved' in any way at the state of affairs. He did admit that his son was quick-tempered.

The doctors presented a solid anti-suicide wall. They said they had never heard of a case of suicide by antimony, and they positively stated that antimony could be administered without any taste in either water or burgundy. Several of the doctors testified to drinking out of the water bottle; but admitted that in the confusion it would have been easy to either switch or clean out the bottle. Dr Johnson testified that Mrs Bravo overheard him mention poison to Mrs Cox. Mrs Bravo asked, 'Did he say he had taken poison?' 'Yes, he did,' replied Mrs Cox. And that was the end of the conversation.

Rowe, the butler, testified that Mr Bravo drank three glasses of burgundy at his last meal and that the half-full bottle was put away. On 19 April he opened another bottle of burgundy. He did not remember who drank it, but the other half-bottle must have been gone. With Florence around, it's not surprising. He had never heard quarrelling, and called Charles Bravo 'one of the kindest gentlemen I ever knew'.

Mary Anne Keeber, the maid, said that she thought Mr and Mrs Bravo were very fond of each other, saw no signs of jealousy, and never heard Dr Gully's name mentioned. At Mrs Cox's request, she had emptied and cleaned the basin Mr Bravo had been vomiting in.

Amelia Bushnell, Mrs Joseph Bravo's maid, had heard Mr Bravo say he had taken nothing but laudanum and testified that Mrs Charles Bravo had blamed his illness on something he ate at the club, cooked in a coppery pan.

John Pritchard, Dr Gully's butler, said that there had been a great attachment between Dr Gully and Mrs Ricardo, but that, in November of the previous year, Dr Gully had given him instructions not to admit Mrs Ricardo or Mrs Cox. Dr Gully had returned pictures, presents, and a key to the Priory, and Mrs Ricardo had returned things to him.

Colleagues testified that Charles Bravo had no worries or cares, that he had made a special study of forensic medicine, and that he would never knowingly take a painful or uncertain medicine.

Mrs Campbell testified that she was met by Mrs Cox when she arrived during Mr Bravo's illness and was told it was poison, while Florence was still chattering about coppery pans at Charlie's club.

Mrs Cox, spectacles glinting, looking middle-aged and dumpy in her black, said that Charles Bravo had told her that she was welcome at the Priory. He had received an anonymous letter accusing him of marrying Gully's mistress for her money. She had seen Dr Gully several times since Mrs Bravo's marriage, and had asked him for his remedy for ague and Jamaica fever, also something to make Mrs Bravo sleep after her miscarriage. Bravo had asked her, 'Why did you tell them? Does Florence know I poisoned myself?'

'I was obliged to tell them. I could not let you die.'

Asked why she had not mentioned this conversation, Mrs Cox replied imperturbably, 'He did not wish me to.' She had not mentioned Dr Gully's name at the first inquest because it might have injured Mrs Bravo's reputation. When she mentioned chloroform to Harrison, she was confused and meant poison. 'Dr Gully was a very fascinating man – one who would be likely to interest women very much.' She said she had done everything she could to restrain Mrs Bravo from her habit of drinking, but without much success.

Mrs Bravo, immersed in grief and a voluminous mourning veil, testified that it was 20 April before she knew her husband was dying of poison. At Brighton, after the first inquest, Mrs Cox had told her that Charles had poisoned himself on account of Gully. She made a full admission of her 'criminal relations' with Dr Gully, but even under a heavy barrage of insinuation, she maintained, under oath, that she was innocent of any extra-marital activities during her marriage to Captain Ricardo. Her protests of innocence were badly shaken when she was handed a letter, written by her to a woman named Laundon, who had been her maid. It was dated 17 November 1870, a date that preceded Captain Ricardo's death by six months. In part, the letter said, 'I hope you will never allude in any way to anyone of what passed at Malvern.' Asked what she referred to, Mrs Bravo answered. 'It was my attachment to Dr Gully, but not a criminal attachment then.' She burst into tears and appealed to the coroner to protect her. So much for semantics.

Then George Griffiths, a former coachman to Mrs Bravo, took the stand. He had worked for Mrs Bravo but had been fired by Mr Bravo for carelessness. He seems to have been a nineteenth-century hot-rod and was accident-prone. But his testimony established the presence of antimony in the form of tartar emetic at the Priory. He had bought a large amount to condition the horses. He had kept it locked in a cupboard in the stable and poured it all down the drain when he left. However, no enquiry was made as to what kind of lock was on the cupboard, and there is only Griffiths's word that, after being fired, he conscientiously poured a large amount of medicine down the drain. It would seem more natural for him to have gone off in a huff, leaving the tartar emetic for the next coachman.

Dr Gully was the last witness to be called during the twenty-three-day inquest. His testimony backed up Florence Bravo's contention that nothing improper had passed between them during Captain Ricardo's lifetime, but when asked about his relations with Captain Ricardo's widow, his rueful reply was 'too true, sir; too true.' He swore that he had nothing to do either directly or indirectly with Charles Bravo's death, and spoke of his chance meetings with Mrs Cox, who told him repeatedly that Mr and Mrs Bravo were 'getting along well.'

The verdict turned out to be the most damaging aspect of the inquest. It concluded that 'Charles Bravo was wilfully murdered by the administration of tartar emetic, but there is not sufficient evidence to fix the guilt upon any person or persons'. The jury significantly declined to use the standard, more familiar wording, 'administered by some person or persons unknown.'

And by the verdict of the jury, the Balham Mystery remains an official cipher. The suicide theory, with a nod of admiration in the direction of a lurking Mrs Cox, does not hold up. Against the unsupported word of Mrs Cox, there is a parade of friends, colleagues, and family who picture Charles Bravo as a happy man, contented with his career and marriage. His letters both to Florence and his family reflect Bravo's unsuicidal, rather complacent state of mind. As for Mrs Cox's statement that 'he took poison for Gully', he had known of Dr Gully's relationship

191

with Florence before he married her, and, according to every witness, Mrs Bravo never saw Dr Gully after her marriage. The only other possibility for suicide would be delayed-action remorse and jealousy, and Charles Bravo just wasn't the brooding type. His repeated denials to the doctors that he had not taken poison, and his affectionate attitude towards his wife at his sick-bed, also lower the boom on the suicide theory. The accident theory can quickly be eliminated. The only place that antimony in the form of tartar emetic was kept at the Priory was in the stables, and it is hardly conceivable that Mr Bravo would ever dose himself in the stable on horse physic; all medicines found in the house tested out as harmless.

Sir John Hall, considered the leading authority on the Bravo case, claims that it had to be both Mrs Bravo and Mrs Cox because they supported each other consistently in their statements, so at variance with all the other witnesses. But consider Florence Bravo's actions after her husband is taken ill. Still befuddled by wine, she sends for the nearest doctor and later for specialists. She talks of food poisoning from the coppery pans at his club.

She says she first heard of poison and suicide when Mrs Cox broke the news to her after they were settled at Brighton. Since she was in a state of shock and did not appear at the first inquest, she begins backing up Mrs Cox only after the Brighton sojourn. So, Mrs Bravo emerges as an upset, concerned wife, extremely fond, talking of food poisoning – then, after the trip to Brighton with Mrs Cox, she accepts and, by testimony, backs up the suicide theory and fortifies Mrs Cox's position.

Something happened at Brighton, and everything points to a little genteel blackmail. Mrs Cox knew her relationship with Dr Gully was more than a harmless infatuation. She knew of her heavy drinking. She knew of the post-Kissingen illness – not hard for a woman with three sons and sickroom experience to diagnose as a miscarriage. And Florence Bravo must, above all, be considered within a specific frame of reference, that of nineteenth-century morals and manners. Within this frame, you have a woman who has made a slip and bounced from the category of 'pure' to 'fallen' woman. She had made an attempt at being respectable again, and Mrs Cox knew intimately the details of the transition. Her knowledge could bounce Florence right back into the latter category. In an age when women blushingly asked for a 'slice of bosom' when being served chicken, and female legs were as unmentionable as four-letter Anglo-Saxon words, public disgrace could assume more importance than suspected murder; and, in Florence Bravo's case, it did.

At Brighton, Mrs Cox probably told Florence that her husband said, 'I have taken poison for Gully.' She told the young widow that if she would follow her lead, Mrs Cox would protect her reputation. In view of all the public agitation, they would have to make statements. The arrangement was that Mrs Cox would tell of Bravo's 'Gully statement' but would testify that relations between Florence and Dr Gully were imprudent but innocent and Charles Bravo was jealous of his wife's past. Florence, in turn, would tell her story of her husband's baseless jealousy of Dr Gully. This way, Florence's character would stay comparatively blameless, while Mrs Cox's suicide theory would be reinforced. And how could Florence say no to perpetrating this half-truth, when the entire truth would mean ruin? Besides, she probably believed Mrs Cox's story of Charlie's suicide.

So, Florence Bravo became an ex-post-facto accessory. By the time Mrs Cox threw her to the wolves at the second inquest in the interest of self-preservation, Mrs Bravo had gone so far in her statements that she was irrevocably implicated. During the second inquest, Mrs Cox had begun to panic. She could bolster the suicide theory by admitting that Mrs Bravo had told her of her intimate relations with Dr Gully and that Charles Bravo knew and brooded over his wife's past sins, or she could protect Mrs Bravo's reputation. Mrs Cox couldn't afford to let the suicide theory languish, or she would be in a most suspicious position. Florence's reputation had to go by the board, and, too late to do anything,

Florence realised with growing horror that Mrs Cox was not the friend she pretended to be, but a blackmailer consumed with some dark purpose of her own. Florence was left with no alternative but to admit her 'criminal relationship' with Dr Gully, which gave the illusion that she was still 'backing up' Mrs Cox, while in actuality these two sherry-sipping ladies had come to a parting of the ways.

Mrs Bravo moved to Buscot to live with her mother. Mrs Cox stopped in Manchester Street and planned to leave for Jamaica at the close of the enquiry. Florence was no intellectual giant, but she knew when she had been had.

It is the only theory that can account for Florence Bravo's opposite actions before and after Brighton. Mrs Bravo, by herself, had neither sufficient character nor motive to do the dirty deed. Nor did she have a strong enough reason to act in conjunction with Mrs Cox. She certainly wouldn't condone the murder of her husband to keep Mrs Cox from returning to Jamaica. The weakness of Florence Bravo's character forms the strength of her innocence. To complain, to pout, to shed a few tears, was her course of action – not poison. There have been suggestions that the relationship between Mrs Bravo and Mrs Cox was of an unhealthy hue. But with Florence's affinity for men, about the only unhealthy thing about their relationship was the amount of sherry they consumed.

Mrs Cox, too, falls with rigid delineation into this frame of reference. In our own era of the freewheeling career girl, it is difficult to remember that in Mrs Cox's day a working woman was an unhappy exception, just a cut above serfdom. In most cases, a governess, a companion, or a poor relation who 'earned her keep' was a step above the servants and a step below the lord and lady of the house, isolated on a lonely plateau without social contacts or standing.

When Charles Bravo showed unmistakable symptoms of snapping the purse shut and shipping her back to her Jamaican home and family, it was not simply a matter of a new job or surroundings. It was social and financial annihilation, and it was a motive. By removing Charles Bravo, she could relieve the pressure being exerted for her to return to Jamaica. She would be once again the dear friend of Florence, whom she could completely dominate, and return to the good old days when Dr Gully's courtly charm caused a flutter under her formidable black bombazine exterior and Florence's home and funds were at her disposal.

Mrs Cox, however, did not know her poisons as well as she knew the gentle art of conniving. By administering a large, economy-sized dose of poison, Mrs Cox was under the impression that Charles Bravo would die immediately. She did not realise that antimony was a variable and unpredictable poison. When it became apparent that Mr Bravo was going to linger a while, Mrs Cox had to come up with some quick answers off the top of her chignon, and she was in a good position. Bravo was in an incoherent state, and Mrs Bravo, during those first chaotic hours, had a case of the hot-and-cold shakes and dry pipes, while the servants were trained to take orders unquestioningly from Mrs Cox. It was only after the doctors agreed that it was a case of irritant poisoning that Mrs Cox came up with the 'I took poison – Don't tell Florence' statement. Only when there was a strong suspicion of murder and a second inquest was looming did Mrs Cox add Dr Gully's name to the statement to give the suicide theory a strong motive. And only at the second inquest, when the jury and public were taking an increasingly dimmer view of the suicide theory, did she tell of the conversation when Bravo asked, 'Why did you tell them?' Only Mrs Cox heard these three conversations with Charles Bravo. There were no witnesses except the necessarily mute Charles, and the words were the only indications of suicide. All the other testimony, all the other facts, pointed to murder. Mrs Cox may not have been telling the truth, but she was a fast girl with a cue.

But in spite of Florence's sex appeal and money, in spite of Mrs Cox's strong, decisive character, things just didn't work out as they did in Florence's favourite romantic novels. Florence Bravo died within the year from a combination of emotional collapse, guilty knowledge, and hitting the bottle, never a healthy combination. In her will, the only mention of Jane Cannon Cox is a reference to her as the mother of three boys to whom Florence Bravo left bequests of £1,000 each. Dr Gully, his name removed from the rosters of all medical societies, died seven years later, full of age, if not honour. And Mrs Cox was last heard of beside a sick-bed in Jamaica, a bad place for her.

Of course, no one actually saw Mrs Cox sneak antimony from the stable. No one saw her toying with Mr Bravo's burgundy decanter or water bottle, but she was the only person involved in the Balham Mystery who had the character, the opportunity, the motive, and an abiding faith that the Lord helps them that help themselves.

The jury at the inquest voiced their opinion in the damning phraseology of the verdict. The man in the street borrowed some meter from Oliver Goldsmith and circulated their own, less carefully phrased verdict:

> *When lovely woman stoops to folly*
> *And finds her husband in the way,*
> *What charm can soothe her melancholy?*
> *What art can turn him into clay?*
>
> *The only means her aims to cover,*
> *And save herself from prison locks,*
> *And repossess her ancient lover*
> *Are burgundy and Mrs Cox.*

It's a little hard on Dr Gully and Florence Bravo, but gratifying to see Mrs Cox getting public recognition for all her work and effort.

# Frankie, Yes – But Johnny?
## Jonathan Goodman

According to a collector of 'Frankie and Albert (or Johnny)' songs,[1] there are more than a hundred versions of the lyric. The origin of the protean lyric-tale is subject to debate. Some say that it was inspired by the shooting of Allen Britt, an eighteen-year-old Negro, by Frankie Baker, a mulatto woman with whom he was living, which happened in St Louis, Missouri, on 15 October 1899; Britt died four days later. Frankie Baker testified that he threatened her with a knife and that she fired at him in self-defence. In 1939, Miss Baker, 'the proprietor of a shoe-shine place', brought an action for $200,000 damages against Republic Pictures for defaming her character and invading her privacy in a film based on the song. During the case, which was eventually dismissed in 1942, she claimed that there were no 'Frankie and Johnny' songs until after she killed Britt. There appears to be evidence, however, that the song has a longer history: Orrick Johns[2] claims that it originated with Mammy Lou, 'a blues singer at Babe Connors' high-brown bawdy-house in St Louis', in the early 1890s, and that Mammy Lou sang it for Paderewski; another belief is that Frankie was Frankie Silver, a white woman who murdered her husband at Toe River, North Carolina, as far back as 1831.[3] But everyone seems to agree that Albert was rechristened Johnny by the Leighton Brothers, a vaudeville act, in 1911.

[1]George Milburn, quoted in Ozark Folk Songs, edited by Vance Randolph, The State Historical Society of Missouri, 1948.
[2]The Time of Our Lives, Stackpole, New York, 1937.
[3]Bulletin of the Folk-Song Society of the Northeast, No. 10, 1935.

This is one of the pre-Johnny versions:

*Frankie was a good girl,*
*Everybody knows,*
*She paid half a hundred*
*For Albert a suit of clothes,*
*He is my man, but he won't come home.*

*Way down in some dark alley*
*I heard a bulldog bark,*
*I believe to my soul my honey*
*Is lost out in the dark,*
*He is my man, but he won't come home.*

*Frankie went uptown this morning,*
*She did not go for fun,*
*Under her apron she carried*
*Albert's forty-one;*
*He is my man, but he won't come home.*

*Frankie went to a bartender,*
*Called for a bottle of beer,*
*Asked him, my loving Albert,*
*Have you see him here?*
*He is my man, but he won't come home.*

*Bartender said to Frankie,*
*I can't tell you a lie,*
*He left here about an hour ago*
*With a girl called Alice Bly,*
*He is your man, but he's doing you wrong.*

*Frankie went up Fourth Street,*
*Came back down on Main,*
*Looking up on the second floor,*
*Saw Albert in another girl's arms;*
*Saying he's my man, but he's doing me wrong.*

*Frankie says to Albert,*
*Baby, don't you run!*

If you don't come to the one you love
I'll shoot you with your own gun,
You are my man, but you're doing me wrong.

Frankie, she shot Albert,
He fell upon the floor,
Says, turn me over easy,
And turn me over slow,
I'm your man, but you shot me down.

Early the next morning,
Just about half-past four,
Eighteen inches of black crêpe
Was hanging on Frankie's door;
Saying he was my man, but he wouldn't come home.

Frankie went over to Mis' Moodie's,
Fell upon her knees,
Says, forgive me, Mis' Moodie,
Forgive me, oh do, please.
How can I when he's my only son?

Frankie went down to the graveyard,
Po-lice by her side,
When she saw the one she loved,
She hollered and she cried,
He was my man, but he wouldn't come home.

Po-lice said to Frankie,
No use to holler and cry,
When you shot the one you loved,
You meant for him to die,
He's your man, but he's dead and gone.

Rubber-tyred buggy,
Silver-mounted hack,
Took Albert to the graveyard
But couldn't bring him back;
He was my man, but he wouldn't come home.

# Acknowledgements and Sources

In addition to those given in the text: 'The Lady's Not for Spurning' is published by permission of the author; 'Mrs Costello Cleans the Boiler' is from *More Studies in Murder* (Harrison Smith & Robert Haas, New York, 1936); 'The Widow of Windy Nook' is published by permission of the author; 'The Medea of Kew Gardens Hills' is published by permission of the author; 'A Slight Case of Arsenical Poisoning', which first appeared in the *Manchester Evening News*, is published by permission of the author; 'The Carew Case' is from *Feminine Frailty* (Ernest Benn, London, 1929); 'The Girl With the Golden Hair' is from *Murder Mysteries of New York* (William Farquhar Payson, New York, 1932); 'A Particular Bed of Dahlias' is from *Studies of French Criminals of the Nineteenth Century* (William Heinemann, London, 1901); 'The Murderer Was a Lady' is © 1949 *Prairie Schooner*, University of Nebraska, Lincoln, Nebraska; 'And to Hell with Burgundy', from *Blood in the Parlour* (A. S. Barnes, New York, 1964), is published by permission of Oak Tree Publications, Inc.; 'Frankie, Yes – But Johnny?', an adapted extract from *Bloody Versicles: The Rhymes of Crime* (David & Charles, Newton Abbot, 1971), is published by permission of the author.